MARTIN CLASSICAL LECTURES

MARTIN CLASSICAL LECTURES

VOLUME XXI

The Martin Classical Lectures are delivered annually
at Oberlin College on a foundation established
by his many friends in honor of Charles Beebe Martin,
for forty-five years a teacher of classical literature
and classical art in Oberlin.

THE MEANING
OF STOICISM

by Ludwig Edelstein

PUBLISHED FOR OBERLIN COLLEGE

BY HARVARD UNIVERSITY PRESS

CAMBRIDGE, MASSACHUSETTS · 1966

PREFATORY NOTE

The late Professor Edelstein delivered the following lectures on "The Meaning of Stoicism" at Oberlin College, under the auspices of the Charles Beebe Martin Lectureship, in April of 1956. The lectures were enthusiastically received by the Oberlin audience, and the committee was eager to publish them as soon as possible. Professor Edelstein, however, wished to take time to equip the text with extensive notes and further discussion of details, but was prevented from carrying out this project by other duties and personal difficulties. After Professor Edelstein's death in August of 1965, the manuscript of his lectures was found among his papers by Professor Harold Cherniss, of the Institute for Advanced Study. The Martin Lectureship Committee is happy and proud to present the text of these lectures substantially as they were delivered in 1956. We regret that Professor Edelstein was not able to complete the project in the fuller form that he had planned; but we believe he would be not unwilling to have the lectures given to the public in their present form. We share with all classicists a feeling of sorrow and loss at his death.

We also wish to thank Professor Cherniss for his courtesy and kindness in making this manuscript available to us for publication in the Martin Lecture series, and Dr. Josiah B. Gould, Jr., of the Claremont Graduate School, for reading proof and preparing the index.

The Martin Lectureship Committee
Oberlin College
Charles T. Murphy, Chairman

PREFACE

He who is privileged to be one of the Martin Lecturers
fortunately does not have to give an elaborate justification
for choosing a classical topic as his theme. Professor Martin, after whom these lectures are named, was himself a
lover of the classics, and the Martin Lecturer is expected
to speak on some aspect of the heritage left to later ages
by Greece and Rome. But perhaps I owe you an explanation for selecting as my subject the philosophy of the
ancients rather than their art or literature or humanism,
as did those who spoke before me, and especially for
selecting among the ancient philosophic systems that of
the Stoics rather than one of the systems formulated by the
leaders of Greek thought, by the Presocratics, Plato, or
Aristotle.

That Greek philosophy, historically considered, is as
great an achievement as Greek tragedy or lyric or history
or architecture I take it you will not deny. Yet, is Greek
philosophy as much alive or meaningful today as are
Greek literature and art, and therefore as worthy of discussion? Even if it is true that all European philosophy
consists of a series of footnotes to Plato, we should, in a
way, be more interested in the last footnote than in the
original text. For the questions of today surely can be

answered only in the language and in the spirit of today.
And have not modern historical method and modern historical consciousness tended to make even more apparent
the essential difference of all ancient thought from the
thought of men influenced by the Jewish-Christian tradition and by the rise of material and intellectual forces of
which antiquity knew nothing?

Yet, although we are so conscious of the historicity even
of philosophical knowledge, or perhaps rather just because
of this historical consciousness, it is hardly possible to
understand ourselves without understanding the past. How
else could one see the peculiarity of our situation, or even
be sure that it is a unique one? And no one would, I
suppose, be so rash as to gainsay that, as a matter of historical record, mankind's attitude toward the universe and
toward society in the past was largely shaped by interpretations of the human situation which were proposed by the
Greeks.

Moreover, one cannot overlook the fact that ancient
ideas survive in our midst. The revival of Thomism is also
a revival of Aristotelianism. Whitehead's lecture on "The
Idea of the Good," in which he gives the quintessence
of his philosophy, is Platonic not merely in its title.
Nietzsche's naturalism and many another naturalism are
revolts against the rationalism embodied in the Platonic
tradition and attempts to return to Presocratic thought.
The study of Greek philosophy no less than the study of
Greek literature or fine arts, it would seem, is more than an
exercise in antiquarianism. In philosophy too the Greek approach has not yet lost its paradigmatic value.

Granted that this is so, however, why do I not speak
about the Presocratics or about Plato or Aristotle, about
the truly great thinkers of antiquity? Why do I propose to
talk about Stoicism, a philosophy of secondary importance,

as is usually maintained, a derivative philosophy of little
or no originality, harking back to the Presocratics, to Plato,
and to Aristotle? The Stoic sage, one of the greatest American Platonists and humanists has contended, is nothing
but "the stony similitude of a Platonist." * To deal with
Stoicism may indeed seem like indulging in mere erudi-
tion, in a performance of interest to the specialist perhaps
but to no one else.

But to consider Stoicism merely a kind of decayed
Platonism, or to reject it as unoriginal and unimportant,
merely echoes the prejudice of the nineteenth century, of
that classicism which sees in everything the Greeks did
after the time of Alexander the Great nothing but symp-
toms of the decline and fall of Greece. The system which
Zeno outlined at the end of the fourth century, which
Cleanthes and Chrysippus, his successors, perfected in the
third century, which Panaetius and Posidonius, the friends
of Scipio and Cicero, reformed in the second and first centuries, and which survives in the works of Cicero, Seneca,
Epictetus, and Marcus Aurelius, the emperor of the second
century after Christ—this system, as patient research of the
past few decades has irrefutably shown, is more than a
bad copy of a splendid original. Like all Hellenistic philosophies it is, moreover, whether for better or for worse,
nearer to the subjective tendency of modern thought than
is the classical realism of Plato or of Aristotle; and its historical influence is not inferior to that of any of its classical
rivals. I need hardly stress the significance that Stoicism
had in antiquity, in the Hellenistic age, and even in the
last centuries of pagan civilization, for speculative and
scientific thought as well as moral and political activity.
Stoic ideas from the very beginning permeated Christian

* Paul Shorey, *Platonism Ancient and Modern* (Berkeley, 1938), p. 23
(quoting a Victorian critic).

teaching. Seneca and Epictetus were regarded as Christians by nature, as it were, though they had been deprived of Christian revelation. If Stoic philosophy was of little importance for the Middle Ages, it came to the fore during the Renaissance. The fight about natural theology and natural law is fought in categories of the Stoa. Stoic ethics and Stoic epistemology are of great concern to the generations from Descartes to Hume. The French Epigrammatists draw from Stoic sources and so do the essayists, men like Montaigne and his successors. The Renaissance drama as well as the tragedies of Shakespeare represent a heroic ideal derived from Stoicism. European humanism from Petrarch to Erasmus and to Matthew Arnold is imbued with Stoic thought. It was only yesterday that John Stuart Mill praised the Stoics. And today their creed is glorified by Albert Schweitzer.* Housman's poems have not without reason been called a version of Seneca's Stoicism.

I trust, then, that the past and present justify my attempt to speak about the Stoa rather than about Plato or Aristotle. Indeed, like the latter, introducing a subject not quite fashionable in his time and yet important, I venture to quote the words which Heraclitus, the revered master of the Stoics, addressed to some visitors who came to call on him and, seeing him in the kitchen warming himself at the stove, hesitated to enter: "Come in; don't be afraid: there are gods even here." †

I also trust that my approach to the subject, though somewhat unfashionable, is not unwarranted. I propose to define the meaning of Stoicism. It is the merit of the most recent investigations that they expatiate on the achievements of the several Stoic philosophers and stress the differences of their several "Stoicisms." Though inter-

* See P. Barth, *Die Stoa,* 6th ed. (Stuttgart, 1946), p. 347.
† *De Partibus Animalium* 645 a 19f.

preters in the nineteenth and early twentieth centuries
were still of the opinion that the lack of material made
it impossible to give an account of the individual systems,
there has of late been worked out a view of the Old Stoa,
the Middle Stoa, and the Late Stoa. Scholars have studied
the few works preserved in their entirety, those of Cicero,
Seneca, Epictetus, and Marcus Aurelius, and have tried to
set forth their peculiar character. From the extant fragments of the writings of the Old and Middle Stoa the
historical development of the school has been recon-
structed. Such an undertaking was the more necessary and
appropriate because, as the ancients themselves knew,
Stoicism was not a uniform doctrine. Throughout the centuries there existed factions; the Stoics treasured their in-
dependence of judgment and quarreled among themselves
like oligarchs.*

Yet, though oligarchs may quarrel among themselves,
they are usually at one in defending the principles of
oligarchic government. Likewise, despite their individual
differences, the Stoic dissenters remained Stoics. That
which they had in common, that which made them Stoics,
is what I understand as the meaning of Stoicism. Without
grasping this common element, it seems to me that one
cannot fully understand even the position taken by the
dissenters, for there is danger of overemphasizing their
individuality and regarding as private property what is
in fact the common possession of them all.

Moreover, after so much detailed study, it is time, I
think, to ask where the truth lies with regard to the
diametrically opposed interpretations of Stoicism proposed
by previous generations. Is it a philosophy of resignation
comparable to the teachings of Buddha? Is it a moral
idealism, trying to overcome the world but deprived of

* H. von Arnim, *Stoicorum veterum fragmenta*, II, fg. 20.

rigor and greatness by constant accommodations and concessions made to common sense? Is it true that, invented to
meet a momentary crisis and at first decreed by fiat, the
Stoic doctrine was backed later by a patchwork of incon-
sistent metaphysical concepts, a reactionary return to positions long refuted? Is Stoicism naïve and crude; does it
merely reinforce old values, or does it teach a revolutionary
attitude, a philosophy of activism? Is it, as Matthew
Arnold said, "the special friend and comforter of all clear-
headed and scrupulous, yet pure-hearted and upward-
striving men in those ages most especially that walk by
sight, not by faith"? Or is it a religion, the vision of a
prophet clad in the language of Greek philosophy?

In order to clarify these issues I intend to examine the
orthodox Stoic concept of nature, a study of which reveals
the essence of Stoic philosophy; the self-criticism of the
Stoa, that is, the development which took place in the
second and first centuries B.C. and which indicates the
limitations and possibilities inherent in Stoicism; and finally, the Stoic way of life, which reveals the values cherished
by the adherents of the Stoa. But first, it will be advantageous, I believe, to state in general terms the aim of the
philosophical enterprise of Zeno and his followers as it is
symbolized in the figure of the Stoic sage. In this ideal, accepted by all Stoics and defined by all of them in the
same manner, the various lines of Stoic thought converge
as in a focus and give rise to an image in which one can
most easily behold the essential and distinctive characteristics of Stoicism. Once the subject has thus been represented in outline, the details, I hope, will become more
easily understandable and assume their proper place within the whole.

CONTENTS

THE MEANING OF STOICISM

I   THE STOIC SAGE

The fundamental problem of all Greek philosophy, as
Augustine saw clearly,[1] is the question concerning the
summum bonum; and the answer of the Stoa like that of
all systems, classical and Hellenistic alike, is that the
highest good of life is *eudaimonia.*[2] But, as Augustine
was also well aware, while the Christian is given blessedness by the God Who bestows hope and with it its
fulfillment of hope, the pagan philosopher believes it
possible to reach happiness "in this unhappy life" by
himself.[3] For the Stoic, therefore, the aim of life is identical with a life of virtue,[4] and this again may be taken
to mean that the only true good is the moral good. As
such, it is at the same time the only thing that is of use;
moreover, it is sufficient for reaching happiness. That is,
goodness or happiness consists in an inner attitude, in
the good will, as Kant would express it. It does not
matter what happens to man. What counts is that he
wants the right, that he does the right, that he makes the
right use of the things that befall him.

But if the Stoic aims at self-mastery, the same could be
said of Socrates, of Plato, and of Aristotle. What is the
specifically Stoic concept of such a rule over oneself?

Undoubtedly, freedom from passions, *apatheia*. Virtue consists in not being disturbed by events.

Not that the ancients and the Stoics in particular, unlike the Renaissance or Descartes or the eighteenth century, were unaware of the fact that passions can lead men to the good. But while Aristotle and Theophrastus take anger as a stimulant to great deeds, the Stoics question the help passions can give to the cause of righteousness. They are inclined to regard even the good passions as bad soldiers, bad allies in the fight of life, because one cannot rely on their leading us in the right direction. They may also bring us to ruin. Moreover, if one's passions are allowed to have their way, they may provoke the bad as well as the good. He who commiserates with others is likely also to hate others. In short, the Stoics distrust "pathological" virtue, virtue based on feeling. They ask for virtue that is based on principle.

Yet if the sage eliminates or expels passions altogether, if he is not willing to allow for them even in moderation, as do the Peripatetics, Pope appears to be right in saying of him:

> In lazy apathy let Stoics boast
> Their virtue fixed, 't is fixed as in a frost
> Contracted all, retiring to the breast.[5]

If even pity for men is a vice in this sage, one may well claim that he does not concern himself with his brethren. His credo, it seems, is: "my soul and God," not "my soul, my brothers' souls, and God." Let him speak of feeling sorrow for another, the sorrow is not heartfelt, it is polite pretense. For as Epictetus puts it, "do not hesitate to sympathize with him who suffers as far as words go, and if it so chance, even to groan with him; but take heed that you do not also groan in your inner being." [6]

But though such an interpretation may already have

been proposed by Theophrastus, though Cicero repeats it, though the Stoics of the Renaissance found it hard to refute, though it is restated by modern scholars, it is certainly not a correct interpretation. As one of the old commentators states, the sympathy of the sage cannot be pretense or affectation, for it is not permissible for him to lie. Moreover, sympathy is needed: without it, one cannot help others; being aggrieved oneself, one asks for sympathy and help. What Epictetus has in mind is something else. To pity another, to assist him, is as if one were trying to save a drowning man. Standing on the shore, one cannot save him; one must enter the water, and one does so because one sympathizes with him. Nevertheless, one must not let oneself be carried away by the current, that is to say, one must not sympathize with him too much, for then both the one who is drowning and the one who tries to rescue him will be drowned. One must take the larger view. It is the same demand that Socrates makes on Crito. He who is not afflicted with the evil must keep his head clear and cool; he must give sound advice. He can do so only if, by remembering that he is not himself the sufferer, he is able to see things as they are in reality.

The Stoic sage, then, is not like the Hindu sage. It is not true that he does good without sympathy for others. The traces of passions, the scars as Zeno says,[7] remain within his soul. Chrysippus admits the same. Seneca puts it well: "this is not strength if one bears what one does not feel." [8] To be sure, the sage overcomes his feelings; he controls them, but he feels nevertheless. Only the Megarian sage wishes to be completely unfeeling. For none of the various Stoicisms does *apatheia* mean freedom from compassion, a virtue "fixed as in a frost." It means rather that the sage does not allow fleeting reactions to grow into passions or fixed habits, just as he is unwilling to be satisfied with merely toning them down. Moreover, the Stoic freedom from passions only is a first step; it is something negative, and the Stoic sage aims at something more, the replacement of passions by different, sound emotions. Commiseration, for example, is a passion and harms the sympathizer as well as the sufferer; but sympathy is good, and so is benevolence. As Seneca says,[9] all that the passionate man does we do too but in a different way. Affections must be true affections. In the technical language of the Stoa it is not *apatheia* but *eupatheia* that is sought. Instead of pleasure, fear, and desire the sage endeavors to feel joy, caution, and well-wishing. These are the main feelings that he puts in the place of passion, and other dispositions of the right kind correspond to other minor passions. It is not easy to translate the term *eupatheia*. "Right passions," it has been translated, and "innocent passion," "emotional states that are good." Perhaps one might better say "feelings molded by the right spirit." As Zeno puts it, *eupatheia* is the easy flow of life; it is a constancy of feeling, Seneca maintains, characterized by equanimity. These words may be deceiving, however; and all the distinctions I have quoted may simply hide the fact that for the sage nothing matters except his own tranquillity, his freedom of mind, his own internal calm.

Whether one speaks of *eupatheia* or *apatheia*, Stoicism, it is maintained, must be called a doctrine of resignation and of acceptance; and this is clearly to be seen in the Stoic's attitude to the result of his actions. In Stoic philosophy, it is said, man's actions are like those of a messenger boy sent to deliver a parcel to someone with instructions to try various addresses in order to find him. The good messenger boy will duly go to all the addresses;

but, if the addressee is not to be found at any of them, it does not matter to the messenger boy. He has done his duty, and the parcel has as little interest for him as the addressee. No desire goes with his action. Everything is a matter of intention, of an inner attitude, and this inner attitude in the last analysis is an attitude of complete indifference.

If this were true, however, the Stoic sage would really be a Cynic or a Skeptic. The Stoa at no time endorsed a theory of indifferentism. From Zeno on to Epictetus and Marcus Aurelius the Stoics assert with one voice that, although virtue alone is good, other things have "value," a term which they invented. With the goods of life it is as it is at the royal court. The king, to be sure, is the highest in rank. But there are others who hold office and, though lower in rank, have a rank of their own. Even though virtue is the only good, things are to be preferred or to be rejected; and this distinction between good and valuable is not a compromise, not a toning down, not an accommodation. It is a distinction that could not have been omitted, for it is of the essence of Stoicism; and the one Stoic who dared to deny it, Ariston, became a heretic, for it is the belief of the Stoic that if things were without value morality itself would be destroyed. To maintain that the only good is moral worth, says Chrysippus, is to do away with the care of one's health, the management of one's estate, participation in politics, the conduct of affairs, the duties of life—even to abandon moral worth itself. In other words, the Stoa combines formal and material ethics, the how and the what; it is opposed to nihilism, to the dissolution of the law, to the ancient and modern belief that man's attitude alone matters, whatever it is that he may be doing. Even the sage chooses health or any other of the preferred things if he is given a choice, for naturally all things that have value are relative in comparison with the morally good, which is the absolutely good. In case of a conflict between what the sage calls good and what he calls valuable, the value of the latter becomes relatively indifferent to him, though in itself it is to be preferred. This is not a concept of double standards; or it is such only in the sense in which a double standard appears in every ethical system, for is it not true that wherever a choice is involved one value has to be given up for the sake of another? Sometimes wealth is given up for the sake of helping, health is given up for the sake of gaining other advantages, and life itself is given up for the sake of saving another life. Do we doubt that nevertheless wealth, health, and life are values?

Yet the interpretation that I have given seems to be refuted by other statements made by the Stoics and seized upon by modern interpreters, ever since Adam Smith wrote his theory of moral sentiment. The Stoics compare life to a game, a game of counters, in which victory is of no importance and it is your playing that matters, not the score you happen to make. Epictetus compares Socrates to one playing at ball. And what was the ball Socrates played with? "Life, imprisonment, exile, taking poison, being deprived of his wife, leaving his children orphans. These were the things he played with, but none the less he played and tossed the ball with balance. So we ought to play the game with all possible care and skill but to treat the ball itself as indifferent." [10] But one must not forget at what moment Socrates plays this game. It is the moment of the greatest decision when the principle that the morally good is the only true good has to be upheld at all costs. As Epictetus again makes Socrates say: "It is to keep up the game that I

come and serve men, so long as I am not commanded to
do anything stupid or unseemly. But if I am told 'Go and
fetch Leon of Salamis', I say: 'I will not go; I will play
no longer'. 'To prison with you'. 'I follow; it is the
game'." [11]

In other words, within the realm of relative values the
game is played according to the rules. Success and failure,
winning and losing, are accepted in the spirit of good
sportsmanship. Naturally, even here the good player hopes
for success; he selects values as long as the outcome is
unclear. If the play turns against him, however, he does
not lose his temper. He finishes the game and accepts
defeat cheerfully. As Epictetus puts it again, quoting
Chrysippus: [12] "As long as the consequences are unknown to me, I always hold fast to what is better adapted
to secure preferred values, for God himself created me
with a faculty of choosing them. Yet if I really knew that
it was ordained for me now to be ill, I should wish to be
ill; for the foot too, if it had a mind, would wish to get
muddy." [13] That is to say that I assent to what happens
if it is not of decisive importance but shall never assent
to doing anything that is morally wrong.

If human life to the Stoic sage is a game, it is a game
with peculiar rules. These rules demand that in certain
situations the player choose death by his own hand or
suffer death from others rather than play along. The
Stoic sage does not adhere to a doctrine of resignation
or glad acceptance no matter what his fate may be. He
upholds the doctrine of assent, of approval, of human
judgment concerning what should and should not be
done. Such a distinction it is essential to make, and in
this case insistence on a correct and strict terminology is
not the ungentlemanly quibbling about words which
Plato finds so contemptible in the philosopher.

Whence does the sage draw the strength to adopt such a heroic attitude toward life? Surely he does not believe in punishment or reward after this life or in immortality. "What does he gain by doing right? What does a man gain who writes Dio's name correctly? The gain of writing. Is there no further reward? Do you look for any greater reward for a good man than to do what is noble and right?" [14] The only thing gained is that unlike the many or the fools he will not be a thread in the tunic without distinction from the rest but will be the purple, "that touch of brilliance which gives distinction and beauty to the rest." [15] There is no evidence that the sage assumes that "the events of the world are directed by a Providence to realize a certain purpose and that the purpose was a worthy one," [16] that things find their resolution in this higher purpose unknown to men. Those who impute such belief to the sage do so because otherwise his actions seem to them incomprehensible. And there is "no friend behind the scene" as those suppose who condemn or cherish or explain Stoicism as a religion. [17]

It is true that the theological language especially of the late Stoics makes man the friend of God, [18] "so that he follows Him of his own free will." But, if the sage finds himself at a place and in a situation where he cannot do the right as he sees it, then he believes that it is his duty to die; and he says to God: "I do not abandon Thee, heaven forbid! But I recognize that Thou hast no need of me. [19] May it be well with Thee." [20] How strikingly different these words are from those of Christ: "My God, my God, why hast Thou forsaken me?" The Stoic's are daring words. They can be spoken because the sage and God are equals, friends on the same level. Like God the sage has the power to will and not to will, to desire and to reject, in short to master his thoughts. [21] He has in his possession the true nature of good and evil.[22] The sage is like God and distinguished from Him only by his mortality. Surely he is inferior to God insofar as God is able to do more good than a human being, but of two sages the one who is richer is not a whit better. Stoic assent to the world or withdrawal from it is the outcome of man's own strength, power, and insight. The blessedness which he gains in this unhappy world is of his making. In contrast to the Augustinian concept of the Christian, the sage is god not because the highest god makes him into a god but rather through himself. Here nothing resembles the Christian ideal. There is no belief in "Thy will be done." Pascal saw this quite clearly, more clearly than the modern interpreters. The Stoic sage lacks the virtue of humility. He knows only of man's grandeur, not of his weakness.

This then, in outline, is the figure of the Stoic sage, on whom the Stoics bestow all the praises man can think of. He and he alone is happy, beautiful, free, rich, does everything right, is the only true statesman, husband, father. That in his righteousness he is not unfeeling for others I hope I have shown. I do not mean to deny, of course, that the sage in his morality is strict or even austere. He is "harsh in the sense in which a wine is said to be harsh when it is employed medicinally and not for drinking at all, because he has no dealings with pleasure and does not tolerate those who have."[23] He is preeminently the man of justice toward himself as well as others. Wherever necessary he punishes and chastises, and in this sense he knows of neither pity nor indulgence.[24] But just as he is not a sentimentalist, as he is not indifferent to values, so does he not invite martyrdom, willing though he is to bear any suffering that is necessary. He is not a picture of stony severity either. His state of mind is rational joy, which is characteristic too of Spinoza's wise man. Surely the Stoic sage makes no scenes.[25] He is human nevertheless. Zeno himself foresaw the possibility of misunderstanding and insisted that only through misinterpretation could those who accepted his teaching become sordid and illiberal, or bitter, stern, rigid, biting, cold, sharp.[26]

It is indeed a "sublime" and "stirring" view of life which the sage represents; but nothing could be more wrong than to consider him a "monster," inhuman in his perfection. His greatness is achieved in the midst of afflictions which he can avoid as little as can any average person. Horace well depicted the accomplishment of the sage, born to a life that remains open to accident and vicissitudes. Once he says:

> Si fractus illabatur orbis
> Impavidum ferient ruinae.[27]

But then again he asserts mockingly: "second only to Zeus: rich, free, honored, beautiful, king of kings, especially while he is healthy and is not troubled by a cold." [28] Alas, man often has a cold; misfortunes befall him. Yet, if you have a cold, says Epictetus,[29] do not ask whether it is reasonable that there should be colds in this world. Wipe your nose rather than lament the events of fortune; do not accuse God.[30] What did He give you hands for if not to wipe your nose and thus to get rid of your anxiety and fear?

"O godlike Zeno/With aspect grave and hoary brow serene/A manly doctrine thine," the Stoic said.[31] The difference between the Stoics and other philosophers, Seneca says, is the difference between men and women; those who have chosen the Stoa have chosen the manly, the heroic cause.[32] You must only remember that this manly, heroic virtue is within the reach of men and women alike. Even if the figure of the Stoic sage is reduced to smaller proportions, to a more human size, if he is not considered a monster, he still remains a towering figure; and one may well ask how any human being can ever hope to do what the sage is supposed to accomplish.

I do not think that the Stoic philosophers ever doubted that it was within human reach to become a sage, even though they admitted that the sage was a rare phenomenon in every age and that perhaps in the whole course of history there had been very few sages. Yet I should also maintain that the question whether or not man can become a sage was not the decisive question for the Stoic philosopher. For what he says about the sage resembles what Plato says about the heavenly city, of which it also does not matter at all whether it exists or does not exist or how often it may be realized on earth. For like the heavenly city of Plato the figure of the Stoic sage is an ideal. It shows the virtues of man, what he could and should be like. In the Hellenistic period, a period of individualism, the ideal could no longer be represented by the simile of the state or man's citizenship in the city of heaven; it could be adequately rendered by the perfection of a human being as imagination envisages it.

As such, the figure of the sage also serves as the standard by which men can judge themselves. Knowing what men ought to be, we are able to discover what we are, for we can measure our progress and our approximation to the ideal. And this indeed is the great demand that Stoicism makes of every person, that he should make moral progress, that he should perfect himself, that he should be a proficient in the medieval sense of this term. Based on the belief in the infinite perfectibility of man's character, this ethos of perfectionism is the essence of Stoicism from its very beginning to its end. Conscious moral growth is the Stoic watchword. This moral growth is intended to conquer even the region of the unconscious which Plato left outside moral consideration, for he considered it impenetrable by rational will. From your dreams, Zeno says,[33] you can tell whether you make progress or not: the sage is a sage even while sleeping.

Even the leading philosophers of the Stoa—Zeno, Chrysippus, Cleanthes, Panaetius, Posidonius, Seneca, Epictetus—never claim to be sages. Their attitude is very different from that of Epicurus. But if even these men did not reach the goal, what hope is there for others? Hope itself is left. For in answer to the question "what is the difference between Plato and the tyrant Dionysius if even Plato is not a sage," Zeno says: "there is a great difference indeed between the two. For Dionysius it would be best to die, for he cannot possibly hope ever to acquire wisdom. For Plato it is best to live, for he can still hope to become a sage." [34] Surely man, being what he is, cannot expect to reach perfection except "late in life and at the setting of life's sun." [35] This moral idealism and optimism is the contribution of the Stoa, this insistence always to work toward the goal, to believe the ideal within reach, to say: "if I am not Socrates yet, I ought to live as one seeking to be Socrates." [36]

How was it that this new ideal arose? What are the motivating forces behind it? The connection of Stoicism with earlier philosophies and especially with that of Socrates is obvious and is confirmed by many of the sayings that I have quoted. But what is new in these is not less. Where does it come from? Almost all interpreters agree that the novel aspect of Stoicism is determined by the particular political and historical situation prevailing at the end of the fourth century B.C. It was a time of

moral and political dissolution. The values of the city-
state and the old religious ideals had broken down; and
a new foundation of life had to be established. The fears
of men had to be allayed; their desires had to be re-
strained.[37]

But how much can be explained in this way? The turn
from the fifth century to the fourth century also marked
a crisis, and it is hard to say whether this crisis was not
a greater one than the crisis at the end of the fourth
century. At any rate, the answer to the earlier crisis was
Platonic idealism. Could it not have been the answer also
to the crisis of the fourth century? Moreover, if an answer
was sought for, Stoicism was not the only answer given.
The philosophy of Epicurus also allays fears and restrains
desires, but in what a different manner! Nevertheless, if
there was a "desperate emergency," [38] Epicurus faced it
also, and he no less than Zeno solved the problem for the
individual human being.

No, if there is one particular feature of Stoicism that
is influenced by the situation, it is one that Stoicism has
in common with Epicureanism. I mean the new consciousness of man's power that arose in the fourth century, the
belief in the deification of the human being. A few years
after Zeno came to Athens in 307 he could hear the
Athenians welcoming Demetrius Poliorcetes, one of the
successors of Alexander the Great. A contemporary historian has described what happened. When Demetrius
returned to Athens from Leucas and Corcyra, the Athenians welcomed him not only with offerings of incense
and crowns and libations but processional choruses also;
and, as they took their places in the crowd, they sang
repeatedly the refrain "that he was the only true god—
son of Poseidon and Aphrodite—while all the others were
asleep or making a journey, or nonexistent." [39] The living

god in human shape had taken the place of the god made of stone or gold or ivory.

But what kind of men were these new gods? One can at least say how the Cynics thought of them, the philosophers with whom Zeno had first studied, or what they thought of the generation preceding these conquistadores and so similar to them. "Philip and his companions . . . lived always plundering, always squandering . . . his companions consisted of men specially selected from all Greece, not for good qualities, but the reverse. Never has history known of such wild beasts. Nature meant them for murderers, but their habits turned them into prostitutes." [40] To be of such a character, "it would seem, is the road to success, fame, and wide-flung empire." And what about Alexander, the great king from whom the Stoics are by many supposed to have inherited their dream of a world state and of the unity of mankind? In him the covetousness of man had found its highest expression. "Alexander," says Seneca, "although he stood upon the shore of the Indian Ocean had need of more territory than he had passed through. It was a man in need who pushed his arms beyond the bounds of nature, who, driven on by reckless greed, plunged headlong into an unexplored and boundless sea . . . he still had need of as much as he still coveted." All things are the sage's; he is not content with a little, but things are not his in the sense in which they are Alexander's. [41] For instead of conquering the world he conquers himself; instead of building up an empire of men or of things he builds up a life of his own regulated by intelligence and governed by reason. But surely in the power which he exerts and in the superhuman effort which he makes he is comparable to Philip, to Alexander, and to Alexander's successors.

Granted, then, that in the limitlessness of his demand

the Stoic sage is like the god-man of his time, the solution proposed might still have been that of Epicurus. What is it that determines the specifically Stoic answer, the moral answer? It is said that the moral purpose itself shapes the answer. Long before it became customary to explain philosophies by human temperaments it was claimed that the true explanation of Stoicism is to be found in the fact that Zeno was a man of strong moral power, a prophet, and Stoic philosophy was determined all through "by a practical need," not by the disinterested desire to know. Stoicism developed a physical theory merely because "nothing which left any room for doubt to get in could give a bewildered world security and guidance" and developed a logic to convince others. It wished men to believe, and it conformed to the Greek requirements by throwing its message into the form of brief syllogistic arguments. The shortcomings of the whole system are obvious. One must excuse them, for, after all, "there is life to be lived." [42]

As far as such judgments are determined by the prejudice of the classicist against the achievements of the Hellenistic period, they no longer need any refutation. It is generally agreed now that one need not necessarily be a man uninterested in truth, a mere *Lebensphilosoph,* simply because one happened to live a few decades after Plato and Aristotle. As far as such judgments are determined, however, by the belief that all philosophy is nothing but an unconscious syllogism overlaid by arguments, that the "unwritten philosophy" which one has shapes the philosophy which one writes, I confess that I do not believe in such interpretations although I grant, as one must, that the philosopher may be determined to a certain extent by intentions of which he is not conscious. Philosophy, I still venture to believe, is the search for truth; there is within man a disinterested desire for understanding.

And surely in the opinion of the Stoa the sage is not merely the man who lives for the sake of moral action, as I have pictured him so far, but is pre-eminently the man who knows and never opines.[43] This is an opinion hardly ever before defended, and none of the Stoic paradoxes was ridiculed more than it was. It illustrates the fact that the sage even in his claim for truth aims at the ideal of perfection. Moreover, throughout the history of Stoicism ever since Zeno, and not in the Middle Stoa only, the sage is also a witness of the order of nature, an admirer and worshiper of nature. Investigation, research, or contemplation, says Seneca, is one of the forms of human existence, not merely a refuge or harbor for the idle; and he adds: "because Zeno, Cleanthes, and Chrysippus have devoted themselves to the study of the truth they have done more for mankind than all those who have engaged in political activities." [44] Such statements make it unlikely that for the Stoics themselves *Lebensphilosophie* had been the ideal, that their opposition to those who tried to separate ethics from physics and logic was determined merely by the wish to sway others, that it was a mere showpiece. It is true that the highest aim of the sage is to learn how to conduct himself in life; and Zeno would say,[45] changing the meaning of Hesiod, "He is best of all men who follows good advice; good too is he who finds out all things for himself; for the one has merely a wide apprehension, the other in obeying good counsel superadds conduct." But neither Zeno nor any other Stoic ever doubted that good counsel was to be based not on a moral fiat but on truth, on an understanding of the world.

Indeed the reaction of the other philosophical schools

to Stoicism shows clearly that what they admired or
rejected in the Stoa were the reasons given, the logical
and metaphysical positions on which the moral attitude
of the sage was based. In antiquity it was often said
that Platonic, Aristotelian, and Stoic ethics did not differ
much in content, that the differences were apparent
rather than real, differences of terms rather than of solu-
tions. The novelty of Stoic physics and logic, however,
was beyond doubt; and that this novelty was an indica-
tion of the Stoa's determined effort to establish the truth
is clear from the violent attacks of ancient Skepticism on
Stoicism as the typical form of dogmatism. In the hand-
book of Sextus Empiricus Stoicism is still almost identical
with dogmatic philosophy. In early Hellenistic Skepticism
Carneades had made Chrysippus his chief target, saying:
"If Chrysippus had not been, I should not be." These
attacks are evidence not so much of the weakness of
Stoicism as of the fact that Skepticism was not safe unless
it could refute Stoic epistemology and metaphysics; and
in Cicero's time Zeno's epistemology, still unchanged,
did in fact cause the temporary eclipse of Skepticism,
for Zeno's theory seemed irrefutable to Antiochus. In
short, to treat Stoicism as a mere *Lebensphilosophie,* a
moralism of the heart and not a moralism of philosophical
insight, would be as wrong as to assume that Kant's
moralism could be understood without his revolutionary
philosophy of criticism, the transcendentalism which is
its very foundation.

It cannot be true, then, that if men received Zeno's
message, the burden of which was "thus saith reason,"
they did so not because they were convinced in a cold
intellectual way but because behind his affirmation there
was a tremendous personal force, because something deep
in their own hearts rose up to bear witness to the things

he affirmed.[46] That Stoicism "was the way of faith" is
further from the truth than the dictum of Matthew
Arnold: "Stoicism is not a creed. It is the philosophy of
all to walk by sight, not by faith."

I hasten to add that the sight is an insight that grows
out of the philosophical discussion of the fourth century.
Stoic physics and logic in the nineteenth and early twentieth centuries used to be characterized as crude, clumsy,
and naïve.[47] It is true that Stoic physics is materialistic
and Stoic logic and epistemology are inflexible. Compared
with Platonism and Aristotelianism Stoicism will always
seem to the idealist to be retrograde and unrefined; but
this does not mean that the new position was taken un-
critically and that the Stoics did not think through the
older theories. It was not for unaccountable reasons that
they went back to Presocratic thought. They did not give
up a truth which they were unable to understand. On
the contrary, they continued the discussion exactly from
the point at which they had found it. This truth, which
recent investigations have re-established, ancient tradition expresses in its usual way in the form of an anecdote.
Zeno consulted the oracle to learn what he should do to
attain the best life, and the god's response was that he
should take on the complexion of the dead. Whereupon,
perceiving what this meant, he studied the ancient
authors.[48] In other words Stoic moralism is not a moralism
determined by merely practical ends. It does not secure
itself by simply taking over ideas that may be helpful or
meet a desperate emergency by a patchwork.[49] The sage
who does the right thing does it because he believes that
he follows nature. Nature as he understands it in his
investigation of truth is his guiding star. It is from this
point of view that I shall try to understand the presuppositions of Stoic philosophy.

II THE STOIC CONCEPT OF NATURE

Stoic philosophy, I believe, takes its departure from the intellectual situation as it had developed at the end of the fourth century. It will therefore be necessary first to describe the outcome of the philosophical debate that preceded the formation of the Stoic school.

The decisive event in the development of fourth century philosophy was the rise of idealism. Plato believed that by his theory of ideas he had solved the metaphysical problem which the Presocratics had discovered. The doctrine of eternal substantial form was meant to establish certainty not only for moral investigations but for scientific research as well. In astronomy, physics, and biology the teleological cause, reason that sets the aim for matter and movement, seemed to explain everything. And this force which shapes things is itself not of this world. The idea, the form, the cause, compared with which all other existence is only concomitant and determined, resides in the beyond. To put the assumption here made into more familiar and technical terminology, the universal is assumed to exist before things exist. How things come into being is a question to which Plato provides no dogmatic or satisfactory answer. He speaks of the power of the ideas to influence things, of a divine art that creates the world, of the soul that moves the material body. Whichever of these terms expresses most adequately his opinion, one thing is certain: for Plato it is not nature alone that reigns over the world. Nature, the catchword of Presocratic philosophy, the symbol of its materialism, is of secondary importance in the Platonic scheme.

From Aristotle nature receives a more important role in the idealists' understanding of the world. The universal is no longer held to exist outside and beyond the phenomena; it resides within them. And things themselves are thought to have a certain desire to realize the form or idea inherent in them. Nature, Aristotle contends, is by itself and in itself teleological. She works like human art, like the human artist. The difference between the two is that nature works from within while art works from without. This, to Aristotle, seems to be the only way in which one can understand coming to be and passing away. If it be asked what is the role of the Deity in this whole process, the answer is that it is the love of the unmoved Mover that sets things in motion. God without being drawn into the temporal process directs it, orders and arranges it, just as a general in command of the army directs and orders its movements.

It is clear that in Aristotelian metaphysics idealism has been toned down and has become more naturalistic. The visible is no longer the mere receptable of the power of the idea which it reproduces in its imperfect manner. The visible has positive qualities of its own that make for the good. The supremacy of the idea has been severely limited. Even this did not satisfy Aristotle's successors. Theophrastus in his careful examination of Aristotle's position is especially critical of the Aristotelian concept of desire. If things desire to realize the good, they must at least have life, soul, sensation. What constitutes the cosmos, then, is its living power. The cosmos itself must be a living animal. The primary fact from which philosophy has to take its start is not matter or idea or their relation but rather life itself. In this way Platonic as well as Aristotelian idealism was refuted and rejected even within the confines of the Aristotelian school.

But the theory of substantial forms, Platonic and Aristotelian idealism, which we are likely to think the dominant and victorious philosophy of the fourth century, was defeated on epistemological grounds also. The Cynics with whom Zeno studied were nominalists; they denied the existence of the universal altogether. In the Platonic school itself the way toward a knowledge of the universal is no longer found in dialectic or in a theory of remembrance of things seen before man's birth or in reason that is an independent principle of understanding. Plato's immediate successor tries to solve the epistemological problem with reference to a sensual scientific perception which grasps in reality the common element. One generation later the Academy falls prey to skepticism. The cautious empiricism of Aristotle which tries to strike a balance between experience and thinking is replaced by an ever greater acknowledgment of the power of facts. In ethics, in physics, in biology, empirical studies come to prevail. Aristotle had feared that, if the existence of immaterial substances ever came to be doubted, physics and not metaphysics would be considered the first science. One could generalize this assertion and say that naturalism and materialism won out over an idealistic philosophy of nature and man. Matter and sense perception, reality in the sense of experience of what happens in space, became a cornerstone of philosophy, of philosophical inquiry and insight.

It seems permissible, then, to say that when Zeno began

his philosophical career, the movement of philosophical thought had come very near the point it was to reach at the beginning of the Renaissance. Then the realism that had dominated the Middle Ages was to be shattered. A new understanding of reason and of the world was in the making. At the end of the fourth century idealism had been tried and had been found wanting. A new approach to the understanding of phenomena was sought, and a new program was outlined for the philosophical enterprise. In its essentials it was not very different from that which Bacon inaugurated in the modern era, for in both the emphasis was on experience, on life, on the here rather than the beyond. Naturalism and materialism were the common ground for all philosophical thought. That Zeno embraced them was not an exception to the rule but was rather in accordance with what was generally true.

But if there could have been no doubt for Zeno that what exists is individual things, that the world is made up of bodies extended in space and time, that the world as it is seen and observed is the reality to be explained, it was less evident how the nature of these things could be determined. That this question can be answered Zeno believed and maintained against the Skeptics. Yet how was the existence of individual things to be understood? What was their nature? What was it that constituted their individuality? Obviously there was in things a material component, matter of some kind. Yet individual things are not merely matter. Each thing is one and at the same time many, the combination of parts. The Stoics were the first to recognize that such combination exists not only in organisms, animals and human beings, but also even in inorganic matter. In all they assume that there is a principle of organization which constitutes unity. In inorganic matter it has the form of disposition. In organic matter, in plants and animals, it is effective as nature. In man it holds sway as soul. In all these different forms in which the organizing principle manifests itself it can be characterized as force or power. It works from the center of each body to the surface and back again from the surface to the center. Looked at from the parts of which the whole consists, the effect of the organizing force can be described as a successive movement; looked at from the point of view of the whole the movement is characterized by simultaneousness. To use the Stoic terms, in every existing thing there is a certain tension or tone that constitutes the relationship between the parts that make up an individual phenomenon. This tension or tone exists throughout the time in which an individual thing exists; it is its individualty and therefore contemporaneous with the beginning of the thing and lasting to its end, its passing away.

Each phenomenon, then, in one mode of its existence is the unfolding of a force comparable to Spinoza's *essentia particularis affirmativa*. And this force must not be imagined as anything immaterial. How could the soul suffer with the body, how could there be similarities between souls of children and souls of parents, if soul were not something material? In a way one might say that the unifying and organizing force is nothing but the expression, the impulse, the movement of that force which makes the body. It is a kind of semen or seed out of which the body comes or grows. It is a kind of fire or refined *pneuma* which imparts a certain proportion, the shape which the thing is going to have. It is seminal reason which works methodically in order to bring about particular being, "Fire endowed with art proceeding in a certain way towards genesis," as Zeno put it.

But, to repeat, this is only one aspect of being. Every phenomenon, of course, also consists of a material substance. It is therefore really two things, matter and determination of matter or particularization of matter, something active and something passive. Yet, since these two principles are taken by the Stoics to be material in some sense, how are we to imagine their coming together or their cooperation? The answer is that the two interpenetrate completely without losing their identity. Metaphysically speaking the axiom that two bodies cannot occupy the same place at the same time does not hold true. Body can move through body. Much ridicule has been heaped upon the Stoics on account of this assumption, which is decisive for their metaphysics. In rebuttal it is fair to say, I think, that a metaphysical axiom which allows body to move through body is no more mysterious than one which makes phenomena imitate ideas or participate in them, or one that explains becoming as the realization of eternal and universal being.

Although in the last analysis the Stoics will admit that each single thing is made up of two components, they do not hesitate to find in the active principle the true nature of all things. The organizing energy or force, the leading principle, is the true essence of things; and one may well understand each phenomenon as the unfolding of the energy which produces it. Expressed differently, the leading principle is the divine element in things, the same divine element that actuates the world as a whole, which is a living being too. For like the individual things, the world is made up of parts that hang together, cooperate, and are bound to one another by sympathy, by organic cooperation as it is found in other organisms also, in the growing of plants, in the working of the human body, in the seasons of the year. Everything, then, since it is material is also in a certain sense divine.

To summarize: The world is made up of things that arise, so to say, by spontaneous generation. An organizing principle creates out of mere matter individual phenomena. Their life and activity is drawn from themselves; they are but movements or aspects of one and the same being, the divine fire, of which the changes in time and space or the "history" is the history of the world. Instead of receiving their essence, their true being, from outside, as a statue is shaped and formed by a sculptor, things have their origin and essence from within, from themselves. They are not merely special instances of a general law. In a purely naturalistic and materialistic fashion the world is explained without recourse to external factors; and that phenomenon which neither Plato nor Aristotle was able to explain, the individualization of things, has become the center of philosophical understanding.

Thus far I have spoken only of things as they exist by themselves and for themselves, but things are also acting upon one another. What is the result of the interrelation of things, of their reciprocal effect or action? Here the Stoic theory takes a strange and unexpected turn. So far we have met only material phenomena: things are material, sensible qualities, colors, sounds, everything that is. But when one body acts upon the other, the scene changes. "Every cause is a body which is the cause to a body of something incorporeal," says Sextus,[1] and therefore something unreal, for bodies alone are realities.

The meaning of the strange assertion can perhaps be best made clear by adducing examples. Suppose that a disease, hypochondria, befalls the body. It causes the arrival of fever. Suppose that a black object turns white. It is made white by another body. In both cases the bodily cause produces in another body some change. It is a visible, objective change. But from the point of view of the thing itself, the existing individuality, nothing new is added and no real change in its nature is brought about. Only a certain disposition, a way of being of this nature, is established. There is modification; but the thing's true being, its essential form, being in the strict sense, has not been changed. Nothing is really different; no new properties have been created, but only attributes that are temporal and fleeting. In other words, the mutual effects or actions of things upon one another are events which take place as it were on the surface of things, which constitute passing moments in their history, which make them act in certain ways without alteration of their nature.

The Stoic concept of what happens in the interrelation of things is really very similar to the modern concept of events, the concept of empiricists like Hume or Mill. An event expresses neither being nor one of its properties, but is something that is asserted of being or said and stated of that which is. The difference between the Stoic concept and the modern concept, however, should not be overlooked. For the Stoics there does remain a belief in the true inner being; the force constituting this is stable and has, so to say, temporal eternality. This stable being must be differentiated from the being found on another level and consisting of the ever varying activities of that being in response to other things to which the subject is fundamentally impervious because it is only the activity that is changed. Through such a definition of being and becoming the Platonic and Aristotelian outlook is reversed. Becoming is not a participation in eternal forms or the realization of eternal principles but is eternal reality itself.

The new concept of reality developed by the Stoics is well illustrated by Stoic logic. Interpreters of the nineteenth and early twentieth centuries generally neglected Stoic logic; or, if they considered it, rejected it as entirely

inadequate and puerile. Recent studies have shown it to
be close to modern mathematical logic or symbolic logic;
but, interesting as this is, I am here concerned not with
Stoic logic as formal logic but with its metaphysical
implications. For the Stoics logic always was an intrinsic
and essential part of philosophy. It had material rather
than formal implications.

First of all the Stoics in contrast to Aristotle and perhaps
even Plato do not define things by genus and specific
difference but rather by enumeration of characteristic
properties. To them man is not two-footed animal but a
living being mortal and endowed with reason and knowledge. In other words the individual cannot be understood as the exemplification of the general rule or plan
that is expressed in the universal concept of genus and
specific difference. Man must be defined as that individual
existence in which different parts are integrated into a
unity. And in the theory of demonstration or scientific
proof the Stoics rely not on the categorical but on the
hypothetical syllogism. The latter, to be sure, was not
unknown to Aristotle and was discussed at length by
Theophrastus; but in Stoic logic it was made the cornerstone of demonstration, and thereby their logic betrays
the entirely different aim and point of reference which
determined Stoic thought.

The difference will again be made clear most easily by
an example. If I say, "all men are mortal; Socrates is a
man; Socrates is mortal," I recognize at least in Aristotle's
opinion the fact of the existence of universals, that they
make up the world. I am intent on finding the universal
that constitutes the truth of the individual. On the other
hand if I say with the Stoics, "if Socrates is a man, he is
mortal; if A, then B; if a thing is this, then this follows,"
then I try to study the connection which exists between

things or happenings or try to find the law that governs the world and binds things together. In technical terms of later ages, the principle of the Aristotelian syllogism is the *dictum de omni et nullo*. That is, what is predicated or stated or asserted about any whole is predicated or stated or asserted about any part of that whole. The principle of the Stoic syllogism is *nota notae est nota rei ipsius*, what qualifies an attribute qualifies the thing possessing it. Here the terms are always concrete individuals, the nature of things is conceived "as an assemblage of changing marks and not as a bundle of eternal attributes or properties." What always presents a certain quality or a certain group of qualities will also present the quality of the qualities which always coexist with the former. Instead of speaking of that which is, I speak of what follows or results. Thus, the concept of succession replaces the concept of substantial existence.

Finally, the Stoic is concerned with necessity rather than with substantial existence. For science is knowledge not of the universal but of the necessary, a necessary connection between concepts which to the Stoics implies absolute determination. Everything has a cause, they say, although sometimes the cause remains hidden to us and we may have to suspend judgment.[2] Nevertheless, there is a cause, a necessity; nothing is left to chance. If the cause has not yet been found, it will be found sometime in the future. This is more than Plato or Aristotle assumed, and even Democritus and Epicurus do not go that far.

It follows that there is never a point where causal explanation can find a resting place. No cause is properly speaking the first.[3] This again is more than Plato and Aristotle would admit. It is the modern concept of causation, the unending chain of causes and events. As Plotinus once put it, according to the Stoa things that are later are enslaved to things that are before.[4] For him as for all Platonists and Aristotelians such a theory is destructive of science, for there are no ultimate eternal facts. The Stoics see in the theory the highest expression of their view of the universe as constantly changing, as a dynamic process in which man too is but a part of necessary events.

Before turning from this sketchy and by no means complete analysis of physics and logic to the ethical application, it would be well to characterize the Stoic position in more general terms. That the Stoics began their deliberation exactly from the point that previous generations had reached has, I hope, become clear. Undoubtedly they also went further than philosophers had gone before them, and one might at first glance be inclined to say that the changes introduced by Zeno were very much in keeping with the spirit of the times. Individualism is characteristic of the Hellenistic period, and the restlessness of that age comes to the fore in the dynamism of life which the Stoa acknowledges; but, if this is a valid explanation, one should not forget that the Epicurean system also is individualistic, though it is hardly dynamic in the sense in which the Stoic doctrine is.

During the last few decades it has become customary to trace certain characteristic teachings of the Stoa—especially the belief in divine creativity and in absolute necessity—to another factor, the racial origin of the founder of the school and of many of its leading members. Zeno, Chrysippus, and others, it has been noted, were of Semitic origin, although, to be sure, they were Hellenized and expressed their thought in Greek categories. I shall not urge—for the advocates of the racial theory would readily admit this—that we really do not know anything about religion in Phoenicia, where Zeno was born, or on Cyprus. I shall not ask how the Stoics succeeded in convincing Greeks of their supposedly un-Greek truth or whether there is a Semitic truth and a Greek truth different from it. It will be enough to show, if that is possible, that each of the positions taken by the Stoics follows from their general philosophical assumptions, from the insight that they received from earlier generations and achieved themselves, from the new perspective that the world had gained in their time or shortly before them.

The scientific fact that the world about men is a world of order, of law, and of rules had been established by the research of the fifth and fourth centuries. Mathematics, astronomy, and biology had been established. Like Plato and Aristotle the Stoics respected these sciences. The modern claim to the contrary notwithstanding, they were not antiscientific. It is true that Cleanthes rejected the heliocentric theory of Aristarchus and did so for metaphysical reasons.[5] So did Bacon reject the system of Copernicus, and Plato and Aristotle felt free to choose the theory that they considered to be in agreement with philosophical truth. Once the distinction between two worlds, between ideas and phenomena or between the spheres above and below the moon, is done away with, order and necessity are a fact to be explained anew.

That the cosmic order could be understood as the outcome of chance, of mechanical forces, seemed to the Stoics unthinkable. The Epicurean recourse to a mere combination of matter seemed to them to accomplish nothing. In this too they agreed with Bacon, and they were perhaps more consistent than he was when they ascribed order to a force inherent in nature, the seed or

semen out of which nature develops. Order is not imposed
from outside; it is within things in their own order; it
pushes from behind, so to say, and does not lead from
in front. Surely Stoicism is not materialism in the usual
sense of the word. It is in a way hylozoism, as the
Presocratic systems have been called, true hylozoism,
for reason and proportion are here thought to be con-
tained in matter in a way not to be found in any of the
Presocratic systems.

Perhaps it is not too farfetched to compare Stoic dynamism with Bergson's creative evolution and his *élan
vital*. Cleanthes speaks of a *vis vitalis*.[6] This concept is
not an invention of Posidonius. In contrast to Aristotle,
for whom astronomy is the most outstanding and paradigmatic science,[7] the biological analogy for the Stoa is
the analogy par excellence. It will be well to remember,
however, that in the Stoic dynamism "there is no fulfillment of novel ends generated in the process of time
itself" and life is not "the expression of creative urgency";
the Stoic's world is not an open but a closed one. There
is as much at the end as there was at the beginning;
as much as was put in and no more.

On the other hand, Stoicism is often called a chapter
in the history of the Greek *logos*. It is not so important
that *logos* is here identified with material stuff as it is
significant that *logos* is considered to be not the objective
content of knowledge, not the concept of form or purpose
superimposed upon matter, but the formative power,
that is, the power of forming things in the right way.
Nature, as I have said before, is a fire proceeding in an
artistic way. Now, what distinguishes the artist from the
amateur according to the Stoic is not so much that the
artist knows what he wants to do—so may the amateur—
as it is that the artist is capable of executing this purpose

or carrying it out. Reason in its usual connotation is here
almost subordinated to action or, better still, to the or-
derliness of action performed, the formula, the proportion. In short, reason is the principle of growth. Not that
the Stoics forget the Socratic concept of *logos* according
to which to know also means to be able to act. Like
Aristotle they can speak of the art of medicine as a
formula of health, a formula that explicates itself; but the
logos of the parts, the tension, is like seed. Its loosening
causes destruction, and its strengthening brings about
life or a vivifying of the parts. This distinctive feature of
the Stoic *logos* is perhaps most apparent in their theory
of eternal recurrence. Like any biological phenomenon
the world is reproduced after its inevitable decay. Its
everness, its true eternity, consists only in this reproduc-
tive life. The *logos* of Plato on the other hand creates one
world, the best; there can be only one because there is
only one best possible world, and it naturally follows that
this best of all possible worlds is eternal. Where Nietzsche
speaks of a game of dice, of mechanical or mechanistic
forces, the Stoics speak of the monotony of a biological
process.

And at this point it must have become abundantly
clear that for the Stoic there is no real aim of this rational
process, no real end. The Stoics are not unclear about
what reason wants: their reason wants nothing but realization. Certainly there are relative purposes. The number
of the stars is useful for the universe.[8] Nature does certain
things for the sake of beauty, for she loves beauty and
rejoices in diversity.[9] Animals and plants exist for the
sake of man; [10] and the cosmos exists for the sake of man
and God, who inhabit the cosmos, for the cosmos is for
their use as Athens and Lacedaemon are for the use of
their inhabitants. Nothing is in vain.[11] But all this is true

only within the process of growth. There is no overall purpose or aim; the realization of the inherent force is the end or purpose itself, and this realization is the only value to be realized. There is nothing behind things; nothing for which they are. The world is a brute fact, mere factuality. This is the awesome, terrifying truth of nature, the truth of the nineteenth and eighteenth centuries.

Yet one may very well object: Are the Stoics not the most outspoken advocates of divine power? Is God not everywhere? Does He not create everything? It is true that God creates everything, but He is not omnipotent. The world necessarily includes moral and physical evil.[12] God cannot help this.[13] The Stoics explain the fact, however, by saying that the good necessarily includes evil as its opposite, that evil is needed as punishment or for some other reason within the economy of the whole or that it is a byproduct or comes about even through negligence, or that destruction is like the sending out of a colony.[14] At any rate, the Stoic God is not absolute. Unlike the Jewish God He does not bring forth the world by fiat. This is a very Greek conception, for as Galen says,[15] "Moses' opinion differs greatly from the opinion of all . . . who among the Greeks have rightly investigated nature. To Moses it seems to be enough that God willed to create a cosmos and presently it was created . . . we, however . . . maintain on the contrary that certain things are impossible by nature, and these God would not even attempt to do."

Moreover, the Stoic God is limited within His power and perishable at least in the manifestation of His power, for this is fire, a physical and impersonal power, which is periodically destroyed. In Stoic theology all traces of anthropomorphism are cleansed away even more than they are by Plato, for there is no philosophical theology

in which the righteous may put his trust, and even more
than they are by Aristotle, for there is not even the
analogical truth that God's relation to the world is that
of a general to his army. Physical allegorization of the
myth is here complete: the concept of the Deity is not
merely purified, but the gods are abolished.

I do not overlook the fact that in the Old Stoa and in
the Late Stoa theistic language is found side by side with
pantheistic. But even in Cleanthes' famous hymn to Zeus
the theistic language is mere metaphor. As he puts it,
the Divine is better expressed through meter, song, and
rhythm; prose is not an expression fitting the greatness of
Divine things.[16] The Deity in which he truly believes is
the cosmos, which he calls *mysterion;* the sun is its torch
bearer.[17] Over and over again Greek philosophy uses
religious language to express physical ideas without adopt-
ing the original connotation inherent in the words; and
if the Stoic speaks of God's providence, one must not
forget that this providence is identical with nature and
necessity.

For the moment enough has been said about the Stoic
concept of nature. The difficulties inherent in it I shall
consider when I speak about Stoic self-criticism. It is
time to turn to an elucidation of the bearing of the concept of nature on Stoic ethics. I trust that you will not,
like Seneca's interlocutor, ask *quid ad mores?* For it must
be clear immediately that, as has already been said, for
the Stoic there is no friend behind the scene, no resolution
of individual events into a higher purpose. In the Stoic
cosmos human virtue surely is but the purple on the
garment. Nay, it might be more justifiable to raise the
question how there can be morality at all in a world such
as the Stoics conceive, how morality can be in accordance
with nature. To answer this question one must reflect on
the Stoic concept of human nature.

Stoic ethics does not begin with an analysis of moral obligation. It begins instead with a psychological analysis, if you will, an analysis of impiousness, of reactions that make up human nature, human constitution. The first part of ethics is the theory of human nature.[18]

Man, the Stoics say, is a living being, an animal, and "the dearest thing to every animal is its own constitution and its consciousness thereof." [19] Its first impulse is to repel all that is injurious and to accept all that is serviceable or akin to it. It is, I am sure, an old observation that is here rephrased or perhaps expressed in a language possibly not unknown to Plato and surely known to Theophrastus, for the Stoic's theory is a theory of *oikeiosis*, of endearment, of reconciliation, or however one may translate this truly untranslatable word.

What is meant by the word? What is it meant to explain? Animals and men cannot live without acting, without doing something; they could not endure without eating or drinking, processes which go on as it were automatically in plants but require decisions in man. All decisions, however, themselves require a point of reference, and in this sense endearment is the necessary presupposition of action or choice.[20] It makes us preserve ourselves.[21] It is by no means self-love, *amour propre*, but is love of self, *amour de soi*. In the most primitive sense of the word it is a *conatus in suo esse perseverandi*. Or one might say that the self-seeking impulse is an instinct; it is no more than the individuality that holds everything together, the *tonos* that constitutes it, though in contrast to inorganic bodies and plants it presupposes self-consciousness.

How does it work, this consciousness through which we are interested in ourselves, through which we consider certain things to be related to us while we reject others, through which we wish to preserve ourselves? When we

are young we want this or that. Like animals we respond
to particular things as good or bad, though unlike animals
we are also able to say and judge that they are good
and bad, for we have reason and are able to speak. To
use one of the homely comparisons of the Stoics, we like
cake and hate carrots, and so we eat cake. We are drawn
into a fight or game; we hate to lose, and so we try to
win. Is cake better for us than carrots? Were we honest
in winning? Such questions arise even when we are
young; but they do not trouble us very much, and we
simply do what we like or enjoy.

Gradually—at the age of fourteen, to be exact—reason
comes into its own. It begins to form general concepts
such as right or wrong, useful or harmful, that is, moral
concepts, concepts of conduct. Then we begin to speak
of honesty and dignity[22] and become aware of a connection within our actions, a relationship; [23] we form principles and act according to them. In short, in addition
to instantaneous, immediate reaction we develop practical reason by which we judge, criticize, and compare.

Now the first consequence drawn by the Stoics is that
practical reason must be developed to the fullest. It is
natural for man to have a plan of action, since he is
rational by nature; and to preserve one's nature, to be
an *essentia particularis affirmativa,* to unfold the energy
of power within us, this is the law of all particular
existence.

The second consequence is this: the attitude of practical reason is truly natural. It constitutes the true self
of man. For to persevere in one's essence is for man to
be a rational being, to act in accordance with moral
concepts, since such actions constitute the specific nature
of man. Otherwise he loses his individuality and is like
an animal.[24] If only he sees the world right, he will see

it as his duty, his essence, to be human, that is, to be
rational, to follow the organizing principle, that is, to
follow reason.

In a sense one can say that this is undeniable, for it is
true that practical reason distinguishes man from animal;
but after all, it was natural for us and in a manner
remains natural for us to act on the spur of the moment
and not to reflect or to act in accordance with reflection.
How should it happen that, as the Stoics claim, what is
truly natural becomes at a certain moment what we also
value more? Why is it in accordance with our nature to
prefer reason? How can one factual description turn into
an ought in preference to another?

The first answer given by the Stoics is, I am afraid,
tautological. Since it is our true nature to be rational,
they say, since we must naturally preserve our nature,
since it is what we are, we must also love it and wish for
it. Otherwise we feel that we are destroyed in our true
being. The good is what by nature we accept as good
for us.

The second answer does perhaps take us further. It is
true, the Stoics say, that we are introduced by our nature
to wisdom only later, that at first we love things and
are by them gradually made acquainted with principles;
but does it not often happen that a friend of ours intro-
duces us to some other person and that after some time
we find the new acquaintance dearer to us than the
friend of old who introduced him to us? [25] Man, then,
in a manner of speaking falls in love with his wisdom on
better acquaintance. It is a strange paradox, for it happens suddenly; one becomes a sage all of a sudden, nay—
like a lover one can even be a sage for some time without
knowing it.

The change from animalism to altruism here asserted

surely means a kind of conversion, a reversal of human nature; but it is no greater reversal than the one that Epicurus acknowledges when he asserts that man who is fundamentally interested only in the pleasures of the stomach and the body will in the end understand that the pleasures of the mind are the greatest he can have. What the Stoics wish to say or imply is, I think, expressed by Goethe. For a long time, he says, we are driven about in life doing one thing and another. Finally we happen to become involved in a new task. We begin to like it and suddenly we understand that it is a destiny for which we were born. In terms of modern philosophy I could say: man is able to rise from the level of un- authentic existence to that of authentic existence, from fraudulent being to true being; and we do this when we understand who we are in reality and decide to be what we are.

When such a conversion in the literal sense of the word has taken place through the realization of ourselves, it follows, of course, that for us the only true good is virtue, that is, reason, planning, conceptual knowledge. Things are still things; they have not changed. It is we who have changed. We are seeing them in a different light, from the other side of the river, so to say. To be sure, even now we cannot call events truly good; but still they can and do have value, though their ultimate value is determined by our principles and sometimes we have to say "no" to an event, have to sacrifice one of these values. Yet certainly detachment from things can never be our aim, our inner attitude, what we think about them. For practical reason refers to things and to actions; it is the principle of action. Without the matter of morality we should indeed forsake morality itself. We should also violate the law of reality. What happens, events, the interaction of substances, is real and not merely phenomenal or illusory. No, we do treat and must treat this reality as what it is: a modification of our nature to be shaped as such, a modification, that is, to be handled as no more than a modification, mainly destructive of our nature, of reason. Finally we should surely act contrary to logic. If I say that the good man is good and nothing else, that he is not a father, a citizen, a lover of health, then I really maintain that only identical analytical judgments are possible (for example, good is good or reason is reason) whereas good can also mean good citizenship, good love of children or of wife or of husband, good enjoyment of health.

But granted that there is some plausibility in this concept of human nature and that it is in accord with the nature of the world, why should it follow that man must be free from passion, that he must accept the verdict of reason alone, and that the emotion engendered by reason is the only one acceptable? Self-love, of which the passions are modes, says Pope, the enemy of the Stoics, "Self-love and reason to one end aspire"; [26] and he is echoing the psychology of Bacon, of Descartes, of the seventeenth and eighteenth centuries. But such is not the belief of the Stoics.

An example—as usual in Greek ethics taken from the bodily actions—will make clear the nature of passions and the nature of reason. Take the difference between a man walking and a man running in a foot race. Both are using their legs, but they move them in a different way. If I walk, the movement of my legs is commensurate with my impulse or intention and varies with it; whenever I wish to change my pace or to stop, I can do so; I go where I want to go. But the runner on the race course is in quite a different position. He runs as quickly as possible. The movement of his legs is so rapid that he cannot stop at will. Even when he reaches the goal, the crossing line, he still runs on and overshoots the mark, carried further by the weight of his body. Now, reason and passion are like the man walking and running. Reasonable action leads me where I want to go. Passionate action leads me where it goes. It is always in excess. It does not follow reason but is "alogical" because it is not commensurate with reason. Therefore I must say that, if I am impassioned, I am "out of myself" and am not free but a slave, that the truly natural symmetry of my powers is upset, and I do not go just so far as I myself wish. From this point of view the passionate impulse is unnatural—for I am by nature reasonable and rational action alone is natural. Nor are Pope and the eighteenth century so far from the Stoic view as it may seem at first glance. For what the Stoics mean is of course that passions are concerned only with the moment, "merely with the present" in Bacon's words, whereas "reason beholdeth the future and sum of time." And who would or could deny that passions concerned with the moment overshoot the mark and are oblivious of the overall picture? Or, as Pope expresses it, "meteor-like flame lawless through the void, destroying others, by himself destroyed." [27]

Yet, since the eighteenth century maintains that the passions are the only spring of action and that reason is not practical in the sense of stimulating human decisions, Pope must make passion and reason aspire to one end and have reason restrain passion,[28] a theory which is very similar to Plato's who speaks of the check of reason. The Stoics, on the other hand, believe, as did Aristotle, that reason is practical. And would a reasonable man choose to sail "on life's vast ocean" with "reason

the card" but "passions as the gale," [29] if he could sail
in the calm waters of rational actions, having eradicated
the passions and changed them into the "easy flow of
life," of the life of reason? For to the reasonable man a
road to security is open, different not only in degree but
in kind—if he only understands his true nature.

At this point, however, an objection seems to be un-
avoidable. If this is man's aim, is he not really concerned
only with himself? He may need things in order to act
morally, but these things are mere means for his end. He
is hardly in need of men; nor, it seems, need he have
concern for them. One may even ask whether he can
have concern at all. He may have insight, that is, knowledge of what is good or bad; he may have courage, that
is, knowledge of what to fear and not to fear; he may
have moderation, that is, knowledge of what to choose
and what to avoid. All these virtues are of service to him
and not to others. He surely cannot be in possession of
a virtue serviceable to his fellow men.

Yet the Stoics insist that the sage is endowed with
the fourth virtue also, justice, that is, knowledge of what
to give to others and not to give to them or, to put it
differently, that he is endowed with benevolence and
sympathy. In modern categories, the Stoics do not believe
that if man rises from the level of unauthentic existence
to the level of authentic existence, he finds himself alone,
deserted, facing nothingness, or that he is only the solitary projection of himself into the future, or that man
is but a solitary soliloquizing actor. The Stoics assert
instead that those who are wise, that is, who live according to reason, have everything good in common. Consequently, he who does good to others does good to himself;
he also knows that if he does harm to another person,
he harms himself. By nature the sage is born for others,

for the community of mankind rather than for the small community in which he lives. He can never wish to be a fragment of mankind, a piece broken off. He wishes to be a member of the common body of humanity. Or to express it in the theological language of the Early and the Late Stoa, we are all children of God. He who follows reason will become aware of this truth. It is only those who do not follow reason who believe that their own good is opposed to that of others, that it is strictly speaking theirs, that they must be enemies of one another, that they must remain within their isolated personal existence.

How is this Stoic contention to be understood? Two explanations are possible, I think. First, reason which constitutes the individuality of man, his true self, as the Stoics say, is in every man the same. That is, the innermost kernel of human existence is identical in all of us. Or, to express it in a seemingly paradoxical and yet quite adequate way, when man is most himself, he is least himself and like all others, for the most individual thing, reason, is the most universal. When man is most alone, he is least alone. In the innermost secret of his soul he is at one with all mankind. This is the truth that speaks to us through the works of all great poets. It is also the truth of the categorical imperative of Kant, which like the reason of the Stoics does not only restrain man but issues commands and puts against the onslaught of passions and feelings the defense of reasonable duties. This is the rational belief in the dignity of my own self which necessarily involves the belief in the dignity of others, respect for them, and moral obligations toward them. And it is at this point that Stoic ethics becomes the foundation of all later humanism.

But it would seem to me to be wrong to explain the

Stoic creed only in such a rational and, if I may say so, cold manner. It is, to be sure, true that reason abstracts from time and space, that it disregards individual features and moves in the realm of the common that binds men together. When the Stoic speaks of the identity of himself with others, however, he means more than rational identity. The foremost experience is the recognition of the other through sympathy. For, in contrast to the psychology of the eighteenth century and to many a psychological theory of our own age, the existence of other persons for the Stoic is not a fact inferentially derived from our own existence. We are certain of the being of others; indeed we are as certain of their existence as we are of our own. We feel with others not merely by empathy, by visualizing their feelings in the light of our own. We know of the feeling of others as an empirical fact. To deny the existence of others is delusion. We are all brothers and children of God not because we recognize God and deduce from His existence that there are other men, but instead we find in the existence of others the demonstration of the common brotherhood of all men.

It should also be clear now why the sage at a certain point of the game cannot afford "to play along any longer," why at the crucial moment of life he may give up even life and all other values for the sake of doing the morally right, why on no condition can he or will he do the morally wrong. If he acted otherwise, he would destroy not only the other by harming him but would destroy himself, his own moral existence. He would destroy what he really and truly is; and compared to this destruction the physical destruction is nothing, for in the last analysis man is not body but soul. Throwing away life, then, but preserving himself inviolate he saves himself. Like the god of the cosmos, one might say, he takes himself back into his own existence. Certainly he does not appear again on the scene, or at most he will reappear in the new cosmos that will resemble the old one in every detail; but such self-destruction is imposed upon the sage as his moral duty. As a moral individual he cannot act otherwise, for he must try to be what he ought to be, no matter what the cost. By his death he confirms the truth for which he has been living, namely, that his true being is nothing but reason; and, as I have said, before reason the differences of time and space do disappear. Again, the meaning of the Stoic doctrine can perhaps be best explained with reference to Kant's philosophy. What the Stoic has in mind is the distinction between the empirical and the intelligible character, the distinction which is implied by the acknowledgment that time and space are but forms of sensual intuition while practical reason is the true nature of man.

III   STOIC SELF-CRITICISM

I have tried to outline the ideal picture of the Stoic sage and to show that the life he leads is life according to nature. In this, all Stoic philosophers of all ages agree, but in the course of time differences arose among them as to the meaning of nature. The epistemological problem was solved in various ways; and it is time now to distinguish more clearly these various Stoic theories, all of which remain fundamentally Stoic, however, as I have emphasized from the beginning.

It has become fashionable in modern scholarship to distinguish the theories of the Old Stoa, the Middle Stoa, and the Late Stoa; and the development within the Old Stoa is usually seen as a development toward greater systematization, toward the more exact elaboration of the doctrine of Zeno. Such a view is in part correct and is borne out by ancient tradition. Zeno, some of the ancients say, defined a number of things merely orally. Cleanthes worked within the framework of Zeno's teaching; and, when even in the first and second generation of Zeno's pupils dissension arose concerning Zeno's opinion, Cleanthes reconciled the divergent views, saying of himself, "I am the donkey that can carry the burden of Zeno." Chrysippus too was not primarily intent on changing

Zeno's teaching. He wanted to put the Stoic doctrine on a surer, more reasonable foundation. "Show me the problem," he is reported to have said to Cleanthes, "and I shall find the solution." Of course, this does not mean that nothing new was added either by Cleanthes or Chrysippus; but on the whole their work consisted in drawing the consequences of Zeno's position, in making it more secure, and systematizing it. A kind of scholasticism developed; the defense of the Stoic dogma against that of other schools was uppermost in the minds of the members of the Old Stoa.

With the Middle Stoa, that is, Stoicism as it was taught between 150 B.C. and 50 B.C., in the generations before Cicero's and his own, a great change set in. By Panaetius and Posidonius Stoicism, it is said, was recast after the model of Platonism and Aristotelianism. Whether or not this characterization is true, one cannot deny the fact that the Stoa of the Greco-Roman world is much different from that of the early Hellenistic period. Aspects of philosophy that Zeno and his pupils had neglected were now made the domain of Stoic investigation. From a political point of view as well as from the point of view of science the Stoa assumed an importance that it had not had before.

The hold of the Middle Stoa did not last long. In the first century A.D., with the beginning of the Late Stoa, one notices a return to the doctrine of Zeno and Chrysippus. Moreover, the emphasis now more even than in the beginning is on moral problems. Epictetus and Marcus Aurelius are not concerned with logic and physics, let alone science; they are concerned with shaping the life of the individual. The achievement of what the tradition calls the younger Stoics has been forgotten, and Stoicism ends in a narrow moralism.

With the correctness of this characterization of Stoic development I am not at present concerned. I do not deny, of course, that the greatest progress made in the study of Stoic philosophy during the last few decades has been in the study of the works of Panaetius and Posidonius. Sometimes it seems to me also that nowhere is the dissension among modern scholars greater than in the appreciation of the philosophies of these two men, and it is difficult to say what their achievement really was; but fortunately this is not of great importance for me, for I propose to scrutinize the teaching of Panaetius and Posidonius not so much from the point of view of their own philosophies as from the point of view of their consideration of the earlier doctrine. In other words, it seems to me that in the thought of Panaetius and Posidonius certain difficulties of Stoic doctrine that have always been observed by ancient and modern interpreters alike come to the fore, are discussed, and are solved in a new spirit. This is what I mean by the Stoic self-criticism in the philosophies of Panaetius and Posidonius, and it is as such self-criticism that I shall here consider both philosophies.

Before I turn to an analysis of this self-criticism, however, I must at least indicate that I differ from two now generally accepted interpretations of the changes that came about. It is usually said that in the Greco-Roman Stoa the influence of the Roman world on Greek thought made itself felt for the first time. On the other hand, it has become customary to assert that the peculiar character of the philosophies of Panaetius and Posidonius is to a high degree due to the fact that the two men were Greeks rather than Semites in origin. As for the latter explanation, I shall not dwell upon the fact that Posidonius at any rate was unanimously regarded in antiquity as a Syrian by birth, and that modern scholars did not dispute this traditional view until about 1920. I have already indicated that in my opinion not much is gained by ascribing to the influence of race and climate philosophical views that are meant to state the truth. As for the influence of the Romans, the new dominant political power, on the development of Greek philosophy, it would, of course, be rash to deny that in a new period of history new philosophical problems arise and that the way in which the world is managed has something to do with our theoretical understanding of the world. What remains uncertain and in my opinion improbable is that the new problems were particularly Roman problems or that through the Romans there came to be an emphasis on the will as against intellect and reason, the specifically Greek qualities. New political problems undoubtedly confronted man living under Roman domination. To that extent for the philosopher who was a political theorist the frame of reference changed, but this does not mean that the spirit in which the new problems were solved must have been essentially different. In fact, I believe that it was not. The idea of a world community was accepted by the Middle Stoa as it had been by Zeno and Chrysippus.

In one respect only can I discern a basic difference between the time in which the Middle Stoa flourished and that in which the Old Stoic dogma had been formulated. The philosophical temper changed considerably. If it is true that hardly ever in the history of philosophy has a philosophical system survived from one generation to the other without some changes—and this seems to be true even of the Scholastic period of the Middle Ages—the changes that came about in all philosophies at the turn from the second to the first century are especially striking.

Skepticism and Epicureanism were practically made over, and Pythagoreanism was revived. Two directions in the change may be distinguished. There is, at first, a greater interest in factual knowledge, and gradually the predominance of reason over experience comes to be stressed. It is perhaps not wrong to say that the development which takes place is similar to that which one finds in the turn from the fifteenth and sixteenth centuries to the seventeenth century. Then, too, methodical rational investigation gradually won out over the unbridled experiments of the early naturalists.

Now, as for the Middle Stoa itself, the change that took place can be described, I think, as a change toward realism and naturalism. The ancient critics of Stoic philosophy had always charged the school with its disdain of facts. Compared to the richness of scientific and factual detail that they found in Plato and especially in Aristotle the Stoic dogma seemed "barren of facts." This does not mean, of course, that the older Stoics were uninterested in science. I have already noted their concern with scientific theories and results. But it is true that Zeno, Cleanthes, and Chrysippus were given to quick and easy generalizations of the findings of the specialists. Nowhere in their writings can one detect an independent scientific judgment on the part of the philosopher.

With Panaetius and Posidonius it is very much different, and it is well to remember that there were good reasons for the preoccupation of these men with science. The turn from the third to the second century B.C. marks the greatest progress in ancient scientific research. This is true of astronomy, geography, and natural studies in general. The development that began in Zeno's time reached its highest point in the second century B.C. It was then that that science was created to which modern

science at the beginning of the Renaissance harked back;
and what was important was not just that certain particular results were achieved but that the sciences reached a
stage of systematic perfection.

The younger Stoics imbibed this new spirit of a science
that is thought to be progressing farther and farther by
the cooperation of succeeding generations. And Panaetius
and Posidonius did not merely scrutinize science from
the point of view of the philosopher but were themselves
scientists. Panaetius was famous for his literary as well as
for his astronomical studies. Posidonius wrote on history
and geography. Both men traveled widely. Posidonius
went to Spain to observe the tides and to verify the ob-
servations previously made. One might very well say that
these men too forged their conclusions in the face of
stubborn and irrefutable facts.

It is, I think, in accordance with such a new awareness
of reality that Panaetius redefined the Stoic concept of
eudaimonia, of living in accordance with nature. The Old
Stoa is often said to have spoken of man and his life and
his actions *in abstracto.* His nature is reason, something
universal, something that is the same in all men. If Plato
and Aristotle spoke of human nature as if all men were
Greeks, the Stoics dealt with it as if all men were one
and the same, as if there were really not individuals but
man as such. And if things are the substratum of moral
actions, they too lose their particular being at the moment
when they are integrated into the plan of action like links
in a chain. They too, in a way, become identical. Health,
riches, glory were seen within a scheme, and it is this
scheme itself that was important rather than the individual values that make it up. The same charge can be
brought against Kantian moralism: the only good thing
that counts in this world is a good will. But what is it

that this good will is aiming at? The individual action
loses its character; and there remains only one identical
and unchanging fact, namely will itself. Consequently,
the moral demand is not free from ambiguity; and the
philosopher is open to the charge that instead of providing
bread he provides stones, instead of concrete knowledge
abstract phrases.

Panaetius, I think, saw this clearly and therefore redefined the Stoic position. According to him, man in this
life plays four roles. One he has as a human being sharing
with all others the same duties. The second role is his as
an individual endowed with specific intellectual and
emotional gifts. Moreover, he has a certain role in society
derived from the chance circumstance of his birth; it is
the role which unconsciously determines his inclinations.
There is a fourth and last role, which he may assume of
his own free will. Theoretically speaking, the virtue practised in all these roles is one and the same; but different
aspects of this one and indivisible virtue come to the
fore in each one of the roles that man may have to act
out.

One is tempted to say with Shakespeare

> All the world's a stage
> And all the men and women merely players.
> They have their exits and their entrances,
> And one man in his time plays many parts;

but the decisive point in this play on this stage is that
man play his role well, that is in the right way, correctly,
or, to use Panaetius' favorite phrase, as is fitting. And
man must bring to perfection that virtue which is particularly his and which for him embodies the moral law.
Then one can truly say that all virtues lead to *eudaimonia,*
that all of them are life in accordance with nature.

In my opinion it is certain that this new concept is

meant merely to clarify the Old Stoic ideal. Even for Panaetius the only good thing is the morally good; there can be no conflict between the good and the useful. All passions have to be subdued. Man must follow the impulses that nature has given him, as had already been stated by Cleanthes, that is, he must follow his rational nature. If Panaetius had really believed that the things to be chosen are things not merely to be preferred but actually to be regarded as good or bad, even then he would not have gone much farther than the Old Stoa, for Chrysippus too allowed things to be called good or bad if one so wished, and it was in the same accommodating sense that he spoke of virtue as not self-sufficient for the happy life.

Panaetius in his psychology or anthropology, however, took a step that at least potentially endangered the Old Stoic concept of man's nature. Zeno and his first pupils had conceived of man's soul as a unity. It is the same reason that wills and thinks and perceives and desires. It is, of course, possible to distinguish logically or in speech different aspects of the unity of the soul; but in reality the soul is one. Passions are but a perversion of reason; and, since the self is one, all conflicts are conflicts within our rational nature and not a fight between reason and something else.

This was a decisive step beyond Platonic and Aristotelian psychology and their concept of the individual. The dualism of Plato puts desires and passions over against reason; and, while reason is the true self of man, there seems to be no power lying beyond the divided life of passions and reason. They interact, as it were, without any point of reference. The individual belongs either to one world or the other. Even Aristotle, for whom choice is a combination of desire and deliberation, does not find a principle of unity beyond or above their difference. The individual still realizes itself in action and not in its being, for action is the only way in which individual being exists.

Like Plato or Aristotle Panaetius speaks of two forces residing within man, appetite and reason. Appetite leads us here and there, and reason teaches the end. What must be achieved is for appetites and desire to go no further than reason wishes or beyond the goal that it has set up, and this is brought about by a miracle. Nature is so constructed that, if man clearly sees the aim, the desires cannot fail to follow suit; and thus the unity of man seems again to be saved. It still is the calm of reason in which we can sail and not the gale of passions in which reason is only the compass. Panaetius does not by any means admit that reason is impotent.

It is difficult to say how far Panaetius changed the Stoic dogma in other respects. He certainly denied the eventual destruction of the world, in which the Stoics had commonly believed. He seems to have rejected the assumption that the world is a living being held together by sympathy. Man is not prey to a destiny that can be read in the stars. Heaven is too far away from our world to allow any influence of the stars on human affairs. If the human being is determined in his actions, it is geographical conditions, the here and now, that shape him. One has the feeling that in the constitution of the world, reason did not for Panaetius play the role that it usually had in Stoic philosophy. It is not seminal reason but rather reason as distinguished, if not separated, from matter that governs the universe, though it would certainly be wrong to assume that he thought of reason as not material at all. The soul, a body in Stoic terminology, still is thought to perish with the physical body.

What is essential and certain in Panaetius' reformulation of the Stoic creed? He grasped more clearly the concept of human individuality and understood the self in the sense of the modern concept of personality, though not, of course, personality definable psychologically as "a distinctive individuality expressing itself in actual deeds or in particular characteristics"; but he did see that there is in personality "a responsibility of the conscious ego towards a higher authority." The individual traits imposed on man by the second or third or fourth of the roles that he may be playing remain subordinated to the common role that nature has given to all men. There is a supreme law that governs human action, a law accessible to reason. In other words, the moral law is not a transcendent divine law that holds sway in a sphere of subordinated and inferior events. Even with Panaetius the "thisworldliness" of the Stoa is preserved. The moral law is identical with the law that governs the visible world.

It is hardly necessary to add that Panaetius' new understanding of human individuality formed the natural starting point of the humanistic movement that began at the turn from the second to the first century B.C. Through Cicero's book *On Duties* Panaetius' philosophy continued to be the inspiration of all later humanism, for here an attempt is made to shape man's life in the form of an eternal human ideal and yet to allow for the cultivation of all his individual gifts in which human nature will express itself without fail to our satisfaction and pleasure if we are only willing to open ourselves to reason and grasp the originally good nature of man.

The originally good nature of man—no concept is more characteristic of the basic optimism of the Stoa. By nature man is dear to himself; gradually he learns to love others as much as he loves his own self. Left to his own devices, that is, following his own nature, he will always act in the right way. But one may well wonder why, if man has a propensity only toward the good, he can turn toward badness. Where does moral evil come from? Why is it so difficult to learn to lead a life that is in accordance with our nature? Ancient and modern critics have put these questions to the orthodox Stoic. The reply given is very much in the spirit of Rousseau. Evil comes from without, the Stoa maintains. Wrong opinions and civilization subvert the human being "by nature shaped right." It is the spell cast over us by things that turns us into sinners.

I am not prepared to argue for or against the correctness of the Stoic reply. To Posidonius, at any rate, it was an unsatisfactory reply. Suppose it to be true, he says, how can one understand that children, even if brought up well, succumb to bad influences? How is it to be explained that man at the beginning of time and the world fell into evil ways? No, the solution must be that in man there is not only one propensity but two. By nature he loves pleasure and success just as much as he is dedicated to reason. Passions are not merely mistaken judgments, nor can one assume that passions by their very nature tend to subordinate themselves to reason. Passions and reason drag men in different directions; and, to use a phrase of Kant's, man is in secret agreement with the enemy without. Good and bad are separated from each other not as our heaven and earth but rather as our heaven and hell, that is, they do not gradually turn into each other or shade off as levels of greater or lesser clarity. They are absolutely and irreconcilably different.

For Posidonius this was first of all a fact of experience, as he tried to show in his detailed analysis of passions.

His insight into the true character of the passionate nature of man forced him to distinguish a good *daimon*
and a bad, a rational and an irrational power of the soul.
To live in accordance with the good *daimon* and never to
be led at all by the one that is evil, this is the aim for
Posidonius too. In other words, virtue alone is good and
the passions must be eradicated to make room for the
life of the intellect, or else we do not live a life in accordance with our true nature. But the unity is enforced
or superimposed; it is not original. We have not fallen
away from the good but are striving to attain it.

This psychological dualism obviously raises as many
questions as it answers. Before considering its metaphysical and logical basis, however—for, although Posidonius
stresses the factual evidence for his theory of passions, he
explains the factual situation by metaphysical considera-
tions—it is necessary to point out some of the consequences
that follow from Posidonius' position. It may seem that
he has done away with the unity of the self altogether
and that he has returned to the position taken by Plato
and Aristotle, but I think that this impression would be
incorrect. From the analysis of psychological phenomena
there emerges a new concept of the unity of man. Man
is will, Posidonius maintains. Neither passion nor reason
directly issues in action; but they fight for control of the
will, which, in itself neutral, mediates action. The question is which of the two contestants is to direct the will,
for they are like two riders trying to mount the same
horse; whichever manages to get into the saddle makes
the horse go in the direction he has chosen.

But how are passions to be prevented from mounting
the horse? Can reason persuade passion? Not at all. It is
only by irrational means that passions can be tamed or,
if not tamed, be changed. In the training of man, in his

attempt to make progress toward the ideal, teaching
through words or theories is not enough. This is, of
course, necessary, and without it nothing can be achieved;
but philosphical education, moral training in the abstract,
must go together with sensual means or be based upon
them.

Music is of primary importance in such a sensual training. It is indispensable for shaping the souls of the young
especially. The choice of right melodies means the choice
of right morals. Posidonius wholeheartedly accepts the
Platonic scheme of education, but much more is at issue
than education at a certain time of life. Passions are part
of human nature, and man must fight unceasingly against
them. In addition to the help of music which tones down
the movement of the passions, he will find it helpful to
indulge in vicarious experience. He must meditate on
the future and imagine situations that may arise. Such
pictures of the imagination exercise over passion the
same influence that reality and actual situations have:
they arouse passions and by arousing them also lead
them to the point of exhaustion. The shortcoming of passions, their secret which we must learn if we wish to
master them, is that, bound to time, they cannot outlast
time. Especially important help for such moral training
is provided by poetry, though not because it gives moral
lessons, as it does when allegorized and interpreted in
the fashion of the Old Stoa by accommodation. For the
Old Stoa the sage was the best poet, and no poet could
achieve anything without being a philosopher. For Posidonius, on the contrary, it is just the pleasure which
poetry evokes that makes it useful, for we crave pleasure,
and pleasure can be used as a kind of psychagogic power.
In this conception of poetic inspiration Posidonius fol-
lowed the theories of Hellenistic aestheticians; but, while

the latter did not clearly state where the psychagogic power of poetry lies, Posidonius was explicit on this point. Poetry is useful because it is pleasurable, that is, because it gives our emotions their fill. In the actions described, especially in the actions of the drama, we have that vicarious experience needed by all of us, young or old, philosophers or fools.

It is immediately evident that Posidonius' definition is reminiscent of Aristotle's. Though the emotions are not purged away, yet poetry is considered by Posidonius too to be an ally of philosophy. Another difference between him and Aristotle is that Posidonius would hardly regard poetry as more universal and philosophical than history. On the other hand, Posidonius agrees with Plato also to some extent, for what is Platonic mythology if not the poetry that we sing to our soul to calm it, that we croon to the child within us that is always afraid and atremble even to the last moment of the life of the philosopher? Yet, most of all, the Posidonian conception of poetry is original. It was well understood by the critics of the sixteenth and seventeenth centuries, who were so deeply imbued with Stoicism. "The poet," says Scaliger, "teaches through action what is the nature of the emotions, so that we embrace the good ones and reject those that are bad. Poetical action then is a form or mode of teaching, it is an exemplar and instrument, the true aim is the shaping of the emotion itself." Posidonius perhaps would not have expressed his opinion in exactly the same words; but on the whole he would, I think, have agreed with Scaliger, whose notion of poetry is derived from the philosophical drama of the Stoics, especially that of Seneca, to whom Scaliger concedes equal rank with Greek tragedy.

And indeed, notwithstanding T. S. Eliot's condemnation of the bombastic and sententious Seneca, notwithstanding the claim that it is Seneca's intention to represent and particularize philosophical ideas through his philosophical mythos, what is Seneca's drama if not the analysis of emotions? In his philosophical writings Seneca in agreement with Posidonius asks that the physician of the soul examine the disease and draw it to the light of day, for only then will he be able to heal. Even in his philosophical writings he gives a premeditation of the future through the contemplation of great persons. Likewise his tragedies are a discussion of suffering, death, fear, and courage, of vengeance, and of all the many forms of pain. While in classical tragedy the conflict is that between man and objective fate, in Seneca it is the conflict within our souls that predominates. To put it in the words of Petrarch, "Everything in this world happens according to the law of war. How many are the emotions and how adverse with which the human mind fights within itself; it is never whole, never one, it is at variance with itself, it is always at war." And we must learn that virtue can exist only where unity exists. Dissent is due to human vices.

I must recall myself from the consideration of this topic to my proper subject. The distinction between passion and reason, as I pointed out before, is first of all a fact of self-observation. Posidonius adduces many examples of this kind. We sometimes cry though we do not want to; we often want to cry and are unable to do so. The argument is not merely empirical, however. If passion is a movement in excess—and Posidonius agrees that it is—how can reason be the cause of passion? For reason in itself is measure, law, order; and as such it cannot be the cause of any disorder or disturbance.

Many words are not needed to make it clear that

Posidonius' argument would not have been convincing to Chrysippus or to any member of the Old Stoa, for to them reason is creativity, artistic creativity, and like the latter even the art of nature may go wrong. Posidonius bases his refutation of Chrysippus on an entirely different conception of reason or on an entirely different experience of reason, I should like to say. What this experience is can be deduced, I think, from Posidonius' definition of mathematics.

The limits of the solid body Posidonius holds, in contradistinction to all other Stoics, are existent not only in thought but also in reality. That which has length and breadth only but no depth, the limit of the figure, does exist as well as its content. No less is it true that the smallest thinkable unit, the point, really exists. In other words, Posidonius is a mathematical realist. The problem as to the existence of mathematics had been discussed since the time of the Presocratic philosophers. Pythagoras and Plato believed in the reality of numbers and mathematical figures. To Aristotle mathematical constructions were a figment of the human mind. While the Stoa generally sided with Aristotle, Posidonius voted for Pythagoras and Plato; and therewith the whole Stoic concept of reality was reversed.

For Posidonius there was not only material reality existing in space and time, but another immaterial reality also existing which is accessible to reason alone, for mathematical knowledge is knowledge of reason. Reason, therefore, not only schematizes facts but constructs facts; it is constitutive of them, is constitutive of a reality of its own. Granted that this is true, a different solution of the basic philosophical problems must obtain. That it was really Posidonius' conception of mathematics that made him see philosophical issues in a different light is attested to by ancient tradition. As Galen, who was familiar with Posidonius' writings, says, he solved the puzzles of philosophy so much better than any other Stoic because he was trained in geometry. Modern interpreters cannot be right in their characterization of Posidonius when they speak of him in the manner of the nineteenth century as a prophet and enthusiast or dub him a visual thinker, as it has become fashionable to do in the twentieth century. The man who defended Euclidean geometry against Epicurus and his conception of mathematics as mere experience, who tried to improve on Euclid and to give demonstrative proof of some of Euclid's axioms, who rebuilt the whole Euclidean teaching in a more systematic fashion—this man was deeply immersed in the scientific movement of his time, he was a scientist no less than a philosopher and a mathematical philosopher at that.

As to the changes introduced by Posidonius in physics, whereas the Stoic school was wont to speak of matter without shape and quality, that is, of emptiness or nothingness to which God, the Creator, gives quality and shape, Posidonius maintained that matter always exists in a certain shape and quality, and God is but the administrator of the cosmos. The anthropological dualism of which I have spoken before is paralleled by a metaphysical dualism as clearly defined. It follows that God, who is thought to be without shape, can be altered into what He wishes or changed into what He wants, but He can do so only to a certain extent. "Divine mind pervades every part of the cosmos as soul pervades us; but in our case too not every part is equally pervaded, but only to a smaller or greater degree." Thus a universe results which is characterized by a gradation of mind. The pantheism of the Stoa is severely restricted. The stars are most divine because their movement is most regular. On the second, lower level, are organisms—man, animals and plants; inorganic matter reveals least of the organizing power of the mind and therefore comes last.

Three powers really govern the world: Zeus, Nature, and Fate, Fate being the third from Zeus in Posidonius' opinion, whereas the Stoics in general identified Zeus or Providence with Nature and necessity. There are also three causes instead of only one through which things exist, that through which something exists, the prime active power, and the principle of activity; and each makes a different contribution or contributes to a different degree. It goes without saying that such a philosophy can better explain the metaphysical evil as well as the moral evil inherent in the world. It has been said of the Stoics that "The world to them is the best of all possible worlds, and everything in it is a necessary evil." The criticism is perhaps not quite fair, any more than is the criticism Voltaire directs at Leibniz in his *Candide*. The Stoics were not unaware of limitations to the material process; and their solution is neither worse nor more confused than that of Aristotle's, for whom good and evil are oppositions found in every category, for whom evil is in the last analysis a characteristic of the particularization of things, a byproduct of the world process. Still, it remains true that it has always been easier to give a rational explanation of imperfection on the basis of genuine dualism.

Many other changes also were made by Posidonius. He surrendered the notion of the interpenetration of bodies, and his theory of the interaction of the elements was heretical. He differed from the Old Stoa in his definitions of time and of the vacuum. Perhaps he doubted the ultimate destruction of the world too. At any rate, he held that the empty space into which the universe is resolved when it is annihilated is limited and not, as the Old Stoa maintained, unlimited. In logic he acknowledged as the criterion of truth not only the "grasping experience" but reason itself, for, as I have already said, he took reason to be constitutive of knowledge and of facts. It might be said that with Posidonius Stoic philosophy in its development reached the point that post-Renaissance rationalism did in Leibniz: nothing is to be found in the intellect that has not previously been in the internal or the external sense—except the intellect itself. He also made minor innovations in the theory of the syllogism (he dealt with the mathematical relations of proportion, the more-or-less, and identity by analogy); and with regard to the foundation of syllogistic reasoning he held that the parts of the syllogism are connected not by a linguistic bond but by implied axioms, just as is the case in mathematics.

It is impossible here to enumerate all the characteristic features of Posidonius' philosophy; but enough has been said, I believe, to show that these changes do not concern unimportant details, that they amount to a reshaping of the whole system, that they remove blemishes of inconsistency from the Stoic dogma, that they amount to a self-criticism of Stoic philosophy by which the doctrine of the school emerges in a purified and more acceptable form. It is also clear, I trust, that Posidonius remained a Stoic, as he himself claimed to be. He emphasized his agreement not only with Zeno and Cleanthes but with Chrysippus also where this was possible. Moreover despite his platonizing and aristotelianizing sympathies he remained a materialist. For him there were no disembodied forms, no intellectual substances; nor was God for him merely a pattern of existence, the periphery of the circle, something separate and by itself, infused into the world only as its order. God was a material point, *pneuma*, or breath; God was matter, and the material qualities had existence. Within the dualistic cosmos unity was to a certain extent restored, for in the final result the forces were subordinated, God coming first, Nature second, Fate third—a peculiar kind of monism, if the Old Stoa can be said to have embraced a peculiar kind of pantheism. The specifically Posidonian solution depends perhaps on the mathematical realism of Posidonius. As numbers are in lines and as lines make up bodies, so soul is an idea of form, the form of space in which it is inherent, a harmony of numbers. Even plants and inorganic matter are a form of space though without harmony of numbers. This is a revival of the old Pythagorean doctrine, which had already done good service to Speusippus and Xenocrates when they tried to overcome the difficulties of Platonic and to some extent of Aristotelian idealism. Even Posidonius' physics is Stoic, changed only by the elimination of the identity of being and becoming in the visible cosmos. The power of form as against the mere formative creativity of reason was revitalized.

In physics and logic the principal aims of Stoicism were restated without inconsistency, without contradiction with facts. On this Posidonius insists wherever he discusses the theories of his predecessors. Whether his concept of rationality was superior to that of the older Stoics or more adequate than theirs I am not prepared to argue. Plutarch and Galen found his system more convincing, and the same must be said even from the point of view of a Kantian of the nineteenth or twentieth centuries. That what is true of logic and physics is true also of ethics I need hardly argue.

That his ethics remained Stoic in the full sense of the

word follows from his belief in the leadership of reason
and the pre-eminence of mind throughout the universe
as the form that shapes all things. It can in fact be said
that almost more than any other Stoic Posidonius gloried
in the greatness of man who can overcome all difficulties
by his own efforts. "There are never any occasions when
you need think yourself safe because you wield the
weapons of fortune; fight with your own. Fortune does
not furnish arms against herself; hence men, equipped
against their foes, are unarmed against fortune herself."
In the spirit of his new empiricism he was not satisfied
either with showing the freedom of man merely by dia-
lectical reasoning or argument. The only Stoic to write
history, he made historical events witness to the moral
law. Attacking Polybius, whose work he continued, he
insisted that it is not circumstances that determine the
decisions of individuals and communities and it is not
an inner law of history that governs events, as Polybius
had at first believed, though at the end of his life he
acknowledged the power of blind chance. In the opinion
of Posidonius physical and geographical factors determine history to a certain extent—and there is besides an
ever increasing moral decay, inevitable through the progress of civilization; but at every moment the individual
is free to break through the magic circle of events and
things if he only wills to do so, for it is his own character
that is his true god. "It is not gold or silver that ruins
man, and it will not help to take either of them away
from him. The Lacedaemonians, forbidden to keep gold,
deposited it with the Arcadians and then proceeded to
make enemies of them in order to regain their gold by
war. Some Celtic people refrain from importing gold but
for silver's sake commit terrible acts. They ought then
to have banished not silver but rather their bad character,

for, if not for the sake of gold or silver, bad men will act immorally with respect to iron or bronze; if not with respect to them, they would exercise their craze for war in order to steal food and drink." Such pronouncements are perhaps the more convincing because in Posidonius' philosophy the belief in human freedom is not a cheap *quid pro quo*. There are three really different chains of causations. There are three real possibilities of choosing. God, though He foresees the future, does not create it all by Himself. Of Posidonius it is not true to say that fate leads him who wills, whereas it drags along him who wills not.

Such a position as that taken by Posidonius implies a larger role for reason in human achievement. The philosopher alone is able to establish the fundamental principles of science and does so by *a priori* argument. The scientist, on the other hand, who studies the phenomena and relies upon observation and experience, must remain within the framework laid down by the philosopher. All sciences are based on presuppositions which science itself cannot prove. This is true of mathematics and astronomy as well as of geography, geology, and history. Thus the philosopher has again become the lawgiver of science; and like Aristotle, with whose fundamental principles concerning the relation of science and philosophy Posidonius was in full agreement, Posidonius subsumed the empirical data under universal principles based on the evidence of speculative reasoning.

In one respect, however, he differed from Aristotle and preserved more of the scientific spirit, as this is understood at present, for he considered scientific research to be a process of continual progress, in which no generation reaches the final end. One cannot repeat the statements of earlier thinkers but must add something of one's own, says Seneca.[1] To be sure, there are certain things which everyone must and will learn from his elders; but new questions remain to be asked, and they can never be solved if men are satisfied with the results previously gained. "The truth is open to all, it has not yet been found out. Much of it will be left even for future generations." And even more forceful and more modern: "Many things unknown to us will be understood by men of future centuries, many are reserved for ages yet to come, when our memories shall have perished. It is a petty world if it contains no questions for every generation to investigate." [2] Finally: "The time will come when mental acumen and prolonged study will bring to light what now lies hidden. The time will come when our successors will wonder how we could have been ignorant of things so obvious." [3]

It would be rash to say that every word of Seneca's is taken from Posidonius; but it is surely a Stoic view that is here presented, and it is surely not the view of the older Stoa. Seneca himself takes no credit for the idea of progress which he sets forth. The formulations used by him comport best with the thought of Posidonius, for Posidonius demanded of man not only that he make an ever renewed attempt to progress morally but that he proceed as far as possible and with all the energy at his disposal in the endeavor to civilize life.

To be sure, the idea of progress was not original with Posidonius. It had first been formulated by Hellenistic scientists in the third century B.C.; but Posidonius was able to integrate it into Stoicism, for in his philosophy— and perhaps also to a certain extent in that of Panaetius —the sciences assumed a greater importance than they had had for the Old Stoa. When Chrysippus gave full recognition to the importance of scientific studies even

for the philosopher, he still justified their usefulness by
the argument that they are conducive to virtue. That is
why he held them to be advantageous and like health
and money to belong to the goods preferred. In the
writings of the younger Stoics, however, a new tone
becomes noticeable. The human arts are said to create
a second nature, as it were. Posidonius traces in detail
the triumph of the human mind that has led man from
the most primitive life at the dawn of history to the height
of civilization; and he glories in the achievement of man,
who by his own efforts alone has overcome the hard-
ships and shortcomings of the situation in which nature,
his stepmother, has placed him. The god who speaks
through reason has achieved the miracle against all ob-
stacles that nature put in his way.

Thus the idea of living in agreement with one's nature
—the only virtue that Posidonius or Panaetius or any of
the other younger Stoics acknowledged—is broadened.
It is freed from any narrow moralism. Progress becomes
progress with regard to everything that is within the
domain of man. He does good to his fellow man not only
by his moral action, by benevolence, friendliness, and
righteousness but also by his work in the arts and sciences. It is in this sense that man brings to man the greatest help and assistance, just as it is true that no one can
do more harm to man than man himself. The usefulness
of any human effort, the industriousness of man, is
morally good; and this is true of technical skills or inven-
tions, the building of cities, the cultivation of the arts
and sciences. It is a common effort in which everybody
has a place, the outstanding genius and people of lesser
gifts; all of them work toward the same end which can
be summarized in Pliny's words, "Man is for man the
embodiment of the divine," or in those of Posidonius,

"One day in the life of the educated lasts longer than the longest lifetime of the uneducated." [4]

The philosophy of the younger Stoics is, then, neither eclecticism nor a mere revival of Platonism or Aristotelianism. To be sure, Panaetius and Posidonius agree in many points with Plato and Aristotle, but they remain Stoics nevertheless not only in name but in fact. The criticism of the older Stoa, the self-criticism, as I have styled it, purified the old inherited dogma and adapted it to the needs and demands of a new time. If this interpretation is right, it has two important consequences which must be stated at least briefly.

First, it has become fashionable to regard Posidonius in a very different light. With his philosophy, it is said, began the trend that finally culminated in narrow Platonism. Posidonius is supposed to have been a mystic who saw this world in the light of the beyond, a prophet of the fate of the soul after death, whose characteristic teaching was eschatological and who preached contempt for the body and propounded an ethics of salvation. Or else it is said that he established a metalogic or that he was the first to introduce oriental ideas into Greek philosophy. Of all this, I must confess, I cannot find anything in the fragments of his works that are preserved. It is quite possible that one or another of the notions found in the later mystic trend can be traced to a misunderstanding of the Posidonian position. His theory was dualistic; but, as I have tried to show, this dualism was not a dualism of body and soul but a dualism within body and soul, in short within man himself, and on the whole his philosophy was a profession of "thisworldliness." Nobody did more than he to reconcile Stoicism with the demands of life.

If this is true, it is also clear that the Stoics of the

first century A.D. and even of the second cannot be said
simply to have returned to the Old Stoa. Perhaps it is
altogether wrong to look for the antecedents of this latest
development of Stoic philosophy, or I should rather say
to be preoccupied with what these men took over from
their predecessors, for they lived in the here and now
and seem to have been more original than modern
scholarship is willing to allow; but insofar as the Stoicism
of an earlier period was influential in the Christian Era
the Stoicism of the younger Stoics is of great importance.
The criticism which they offered of the older theories
made inroads. In Musonius' insistence on habituation
and practice in ethics one can see the effect of Posidonius'
fight against Chrysippus. Seneca's individualism in metaphysical, ethical, and aesthetic questions, his concern for
the needs of the individual in education, his conception
of anticipation and premeditation—all this would be unthinkable without the influence of Posidonius. Only in
one respect did the older Stoa keep the upper hand. Its
optimism or at least its cosmic optimism won out over
the pessimistic dualism of Posidonius. As for the rest, the
latest phase of Stoicism seems to have been nearer to
the Middle Stoa than to the beginnings made by Zeno,
Cleanthes, and Chrysippus.

IV   THE STOIC WAY OF LIFE

The Stoic way of life, the expression that I have chosen
to characterize the Stoic's attitude toward practical affairs, is really an anachronism. It was Pythagoras who
first taught a "way of life." The Stoics usually speak of
an "art of life," an *ars vivendi*, not in the sense of any
inspirational action but in the sense of a settled disposition, which makes man act with the certainty of an
accomplished craftsman, which teaches him how to do
things in an unvarying order. That there could be such
an art the skeptics of antiquity vehemently denied; but
the Stoics maintained their contention unperturbed, and
it goes without saying that it is the Stoic sage who pos-
sesses this art in its perfection.

The Stoic art of life can be seen from two points of
view. First, it consists of general rules, of precepts of a
universal nature. In short, it is the upshot of ethics,
which without a knowledge of physics and logic cannot
be fully comprehended. But the art of life also includes
the discussion of specific cases and situations, the famous
or notorious casuistry. In point of fact, this consideration
of particular cases was an invention of the Stoa. From
there it was taken over into Christian ethics, culminated
in the teaching of the Catholic Church, and was surely

not without influence on the theories of modern psychology, especially of modern psychoanalysis.

Important as is this general characteristic of the Stoic way of life, it is equally important that from the very beginning Stoic teaching was concerned not merely with the attitude of the individual and with his concerns. Perhaps it is true that classical ethics taught man how to shape himself, that is, to shape his being as an artist shapes a statue. The harmonious personality was the aim of Epicurus also. Yet one often gets the impression that these ancient moralists thought of man as if he were isolated from others. This is not so of the Stoic, for whom man is a social being and can perfect himself only within the community of man and not just the community of citizens either. The highest ideal of the Stoic way of life, therefore, was to live with others. While it was the dream of the Epicurean sage to live hidden from the world, it was the duty of the Stoic sage to understand that he could never consider himself a private individual. Social obligations take precedence over individual tasks, and individual ethics is *ipso facto* social ethics. Perhaps this is one of the reasons why Stoicism exercised such a profound influence on Christianity.

In Late Stoic doctrine the moral attitude of the sage is represented in the form of obligations toward virtues or toward people and institutions. Hierocles uses a system of concentric circles, of which the innermost represents man and his duties to himself and the others represent his duties to family, friends, and country. I shall not begin my analysis with the innermost circle but shall rather try to observe some of the effects before discussing the cause producing them and shall thus attempt to summarize and bring to an end my whole undertaking. In this way I hope to clarify the issue whether Stoic ethics was an endeavor to re-establish the traditional code of morals or was rather a radical criticism of the moral values current in antiquity. This means, of course, that I must also try to explain the meaning of the famous cynical paradoxes of the Stoa, those terrible sayings that shocked Cicero to the point of making him ashamed even to mention them.

As with Aristotle, so with the Stoics the family is the first natural unity to which man belongs. The sage will marry, the Stoics say, and have children. Was not Socrates married and did he not have children? This is his duty to the community and to his fatherland, which he must preserve; it is his duty to nature, for the eternity of the species is the eternity of mankind.

If this general framework is one which the Stoics shared with classical morality, almost every detail of it assumes a different aspect. This appears first of all in the respect of the Stoic husband for his wife. To be sure, even in Xenophon's writings one finds respect for the married woman, and Isocrates can speak of marriage as a community of life as a whole; but it is really the Stoa that first recognized the full equality of husband and wife. Not only did they hold that men and women have one virtue and that beyond and above the manly virtues there are human virtues which are valid for both men and women, but they considered matrimony to be much more than a community of the body, to be a community of the soul. The wife is the husband's other self, his truest friend. He will, therefore, not marry for money or for family connections or even for beauty. What is important about married life is what it contributes to the human qualities of both partners, the use of their common life. Nothing is farther from the Stoic attitude, though by no means from the attitude of the classical centuries, than the point of view expressed by Shakespeare's Petruchio "I will be master of what is my own; she is my goods, my chattels."

Thus the first step is taken in acknowledging the dignity, the rights, and the humanity of the other person; and what is true of the husband's attitude toward his wife is true also of his attitude toward his children. Their rights must be respected and especially their right to educate themselves and to choose their own way of life. When Epictetus was confronted by a son who did not have his father's permission to study philosophy, he was not afraid to defend the son against the father. The father's rights and prerogatives are limited by the rights of the son, or rather the obligations of the one as well as of the other must be respected.

This respect for the inalienable and indefeasible rights of the individual appears most clearly in the attitude prescribed with respect to the slave, the third member of the family in addition to parents and children. The slave, said Chrysippus, is a man hired for life.[1] Slavery is nothing but subordination to the master; if it turns into possession of the slave by the master, it is lordship, and this is evil. As human beings, free men and slaves are equals. That is why the slave can and does bestow benefits upon his master just as the master bestows benefits on him.

These few remarks concerning family life of themselves indicate, I think, the tendency of the change brought about by Stoic ethics: it imbued man's actions with a new respect for human dignity. One may justly wonder, however, whether people have not always respected the dignity of those they loved, no matter what literary evidence may say to the contrary; and the Stoics, it may be contended, merely sanctioned with regard to family life what the heart of man always insisted upon. Even so, there can be no doubt that in the analysis of social obligations the Stoics cut through all the old established and inherited prejudices of the Greeks.

This is first of all true of the Stoic estimate of manual labor. Whether or not the preclassical centuries were free of contempt for manual labor, by the end of the classical era it had become something contemptible in democratic and oligarchical societies alike. Socrates' defense of the workmen on the ground that work brings neither disgrace nor dishonor is quite revolutionary, and so is the Pythagorean theory of work and workmanship. What is much more characteristic of the common attitude is Aristotle's remark [2] that the artisan is subject to limited servitude while the slave is subject to unlimited servitude. Between the two, then, there is only a difference of degree. Surely, in all early centuries there is no idealization of work as such. It is considered to be a dire necessity rather than an ennobling activity; and, most important, it precludes man from practising moral virtue.

Stoic philosophy attributed to work a value of its own, however. Work is a natural human occupation and does not exclude man from a virtuous life; it is compatible with the moral order and forms a part of it, for morality can be realized not merely in performing the duties of the citizen but also in any other human action. Aristotle had allowed that workmanship may be noble or ignoble depending on the degree of virtue that it requires as an accessory; but he had declined even to discuss the question in detail in his *Politics* because that would be ungentlemanlike. For the Stoa it was axiomatic that in whatever station man may find himself it is possible for him to live up to moral rules.

The Stoic attitude toward manual work has far-reach-

ing economic consequences. In terms of economic theory
it means that the arts and crafts are no longer distinguished as less noble than the possession of wealth.
Worker and capitalist are on the same level, so to speak.
The relation between them becomes that of two rich
men, equally independent, making use of their wealth,
the wealth of the one being his skill or manual strength
and the wealth of the other his money. There is also a
change in the attitude toward the product of wealth
and toward the worker. The classical age was concerned
only with technical proficiency in the artist and with the
product of his art or craft. Now the human qualities of
the craftsman, his inner relation to his achievement and
to his customer, his reliability, his wish to do right in
the widest sense of the term, are made the main content
of appreciation. This point is especially important. Aristotle[3] can still put the *aporia:* will it not be necessary
for artisans to have virtue, since they frequently fall
short in their tasks owing to intemperance? But he de-
cides that nothing can be done about this. While the
owner of a slave must see to it that the slave is educated
and becomes virtuous, the artisan who lives in limited
slavery is outside the control of his employer; his virtue
is his personal concern. Through Stoic teaching, work is
moralized, however. A sense of responsibility toward it
is enjoined upon everybody. How one behaves in the
performance of one's work is no longer a matter of indifference. The moral character must, so to speak, shine
through one's doings; soberness and temperance must
shine through every activity. Thus an ethos of work and
workmanship arises, unknown before or known at most
to the political theorist who can speak of the official as
a servant of the state or of the law.[4]

Most important perhaps, the rehabilitation and the re-shaping of men's attitude toward manual work eventually leads to a more general theory of calling or vocation. The classical age knew nothing of what can be properly called professional ethics. That is, it was not understood that each profession imposes specific duties. For example, the physician must help his patient, be he free or slave, friend or enemy, and on no condition is he permitted to do any harm. The judge is not allowed to show favor to anybody, not even to the friend who may appear before him; impartiality is his specific virtue. These duties are imposed upon the member of the profession by the role he plays in life. When he puts off his role, he is no longer bound by them. The physician who fights as a soldier may kill his enemy, and the judge outside the courtroom may help his friend. Other roles impose other duties, and men play many roles in their lives.

The influence of this concept of professional ethics can hardly be exaggerated. Antiquity had no state regu-lations for the performance of work or the performance of a profession, and there were no guilds like the Medieval guilds to maintain such standards. Stoic teaching, to be sure, was obligatory only for one who adhered to Sto-icism. Even as the effort of individuals, however, this attempt to establish a professional ethics made inroads and prepared the way for the Christian concept of calling. As early Christianity teaches, the monk's calling is a special one, for he has been called by God to serve Him; but everyone, even the lowliest person, has a calling to fulfill if he only chooses to do so. He too has been called by God to perform certain duties. Stoic professional ethics teaches the same thing. The only difference be-tween the Christian and the Stoic doctrines is that where

Christianity speaks of revelation and divine ordinance the Stoic speaks of human insight into the moral law that is divine.

It goes without saying that such a professional ethics is not restricted to craftsmen and artisans and members of a profession. In the Stoic's opinion, business too has an ethics of its own. To make as much money as one needs is fair but to steal from another what is his is against the human law, said Chrysippus;[5] and in the famous debate between Antipater and Diogenes[6] the rights of the seller and the buyer are scrutinized: must the seller point out all the faults of his wares? Is he obliged to live up only to the laws of the country in which he happens to do business or must he always be mindful of the common nature of man and the common natural law that protects all?

Nor are the rich, those who inherited their wealth and live for its enjoyment, left to their own devices. Stoic philosophy demands from them, first of all, that they practise charity. The general ruthlessness of the classical world in which one had to be either hammer or anvil is largely concealed from the modern interpreter because with few exceptions the literature preserved is the product of the classes of wealth and power. Even granted that in antiquity family feeling was stronger and that therefore many needs that now require the help of the community or the state were privately taken care of, it remains true that the poor were condemned to a miserable lot. Stoic philosophy initiated a reversal of the attitude of the wealthy to the poor and infused the ideal of humaneness with the virtue of generosity. The themes of benevolence and charity were treated from the time of Cleanthes to that of Seneca, and in these writings it is set forth in much detail how one should give, to whom, and when as well as how to reciprocate gifts. Sometimes one may be annoyed by the fine distinctions drawn, but such a feeling of annoyance cannot obscure the fact that the Stoic teaching marked a very great moral progress indeed.

Generally speaking, the thesis of the Stoics was that he who has money does not have it for himself, does not possess it or own it any more than he owns his wife or his children or anything else. You have money for the benefit of your children, of your relations, of your friends, or the state, says Seneca. The rich man, to put it succinctly, is but the trustee of his wealth. Such a position was maintained by the Stoics without in any way casting doubt on the right of private property. Private property is a natural good; it is guaranteed by justice, which gives to everybody his own. The world is a theater with different seats, and one must not complain if one does not sit in the front row nor claim that one has a right to do so. Rights differ as men differ. The Stoa, therefore, opposed socialism and communism as they were preached in Hellenistic utopias, but it did not condone a theory of the *laissez faire,* to which Aristotle had already objected.[7] Unlike him, however, the Stoics did not advocate statism as a remedy, nor did they wait for the invisible hand of God to set things right, as Adam Smith was willing to do. Instead they asked the individual to learn that it is necessary for him to live for others and that he is born for human society at large, of which he must always feel himself to be a member rather than a fragment separated off. Here in humanity and not in the state, in the moral community of man, he is truly at home. He must take care of present and future as far as social problems are concerned; and the greatest sin of a human being is to say *après nous le déluge* or, as the Stoics put

it in the familiar words of a Greek poet, "It is wicked
and inhuman for men to declare that they care not if,
when they themselves are dead, the universal conflagra-
tion ensues." [8]

After a man's duties to his family and to his occupation
come his duties to the state. The Stoic naturally is a
law-abiding citizen. Was not Socrates such a one, asked
Epictetus; and, obviously resenting the attacks made in
his time on philosophers and the charges against them
of subversion and revolutionary ideas, he insisted that
philosophers usually are good citizens and know that one
must obey the law conscientiously and in every respect. [9]
Since in antiquity religious duties were part of the law
of the state, the philosopher would also fulfill all religious
obligations.

That does not mean, of course, that the philosopher
will also share the religious views of other men. One
worships the gods, the Stoics maintain, not because the
gods are in need of worship but because man is in need
of it, for he must remind himself of the existence of the
divinity. The prayer offered has no influence over the
gods, but it directs man's attention to the divine within.
The statue of the god is not god, for god has no human
shape; and the stories that mythology tells about the
deities are wrong if taken literally. These stories must
be reinterpreted according to the spirit, that is, meta-
phorically; and then they yield insight into the nature
of the cosmos.

In other words, what the Stoa believed in is natural
theology or a religion within the limits of reason, to use
Kant's famous phrase; and the Stoics did not dream, any
more than did Kant, of eliminating popular religion from
the social scheme of things or destroying it altogether.
They acknowledged its value for the masses. Not every-

body can gain philosophical insight, and mythology expresses in terms of imagination the truth of philosophy. This was not a standard of a double truth either for the Stoics or for Kant. All men agree in their belief in the existence of God. Nothing is more certain. Still, one cannot help feeling that if the Stoic was honest in endorsing the average faith in the divine, he was pretending somewhat and making concessions when he also endorsed the religious ceremonies. At any rate, it seems safe to say that these ceremonies mattered little to the Stoic philosopher, even as they did to Kant. They were devised for the many rather than for the few; and, practised in the right way, that is, practised with the right attitude of mind, they might not be harmful. It is more important, at any rate, to shape one's whole life in such a way that it may turn into service to God. Compared with this aim the occasional prayer or sacrifice or obedience is of little avail.

In one respect only did the Stoic show real concern for religious practices, a concern that was as unintelligible to the ancient rationalist as it is to the rationalist of the modern age. I refer to the Stoic's trust in divination. With the possible exception of Panaetius all Stoic philosophers defended the belief in the science of omens that reveal to man the divine interest in his fate. Since they were so bitterly criticised by Epicureans and Skeptics for their naïveté and superstitiousness and yet persisted in their stubborn adherence to prophecies and miracles, the sincerity of their opinion cannot be questioned; and it is not so difficult as modern interpreters usually find it to understand their position. That all actions are predetermined in some manner and that necessity holds sway over human and divine affairs all Stoics asserted. Theoretically, then, the future could be known at least by a mind able to follow all lines of causation; and if it is true that this cosmos is held together by sympathy and all its members form a unity or common body, is it credible that the knowledge of one part of this body should be withheld from another? Is it not rather probable and even most likely that God's benevolence will share with the human being what is so important for him to have, insight into the future? This, at any rate, is the way the Stoics argued and had to argue in accordance with their philosophical assumptions. If with the ancient critics one doubts their good sense, one can at least not deny their consistency. Moreover, one must not forget that for the Stoics the reality of divination is proved by experience as decisively as it is by reason. They were convinced that the material which they had studiously collected warranted the conclusion that prophecies had been fulfilled and that divine signs had been read aright. Empiricism has always been less able than rational and skeptical inquiry to refute apparent facts; and the Stoic's empirical justification of divination was no exception to this universal rule.

Within the scheme of civil life the performance of religious duties is but one form of human activity, however. No less important and much wider in its application is the law governing the relations between men, the adjudication of the claims that they may have against one another, and the punishment of the criminal and the lawless. From Plato and Aristotle the Stoa inherited the conviction that any law enacted by the people or the magistrates deals with the universal aspects of a case and does not take account of particular circumstances, so that equity is needed in interpreting the law, which must be understood according to the spirit rather than according to the letter. Human motives and situations, since they are characteristic of individual actions, must be considered also. The classical doctrine of equity reached its perfection in the Stoa. The gravest misinterpretation of the law is that which is symbolized in the saying *Fiat justitia, pereat mundus*. The guiding principle must be: *summum ius summa iniuria*. Accepted by Roman jurors and made the cornerstone of Roman law, this Stoic concept of justice and equity has determined juridical thinking down to the present, as much as has the Stoic principle: equal justice under law.

No less important was the Stoic clarification of the problem of legality and morality. Is it not possible that a law of the state may be morally wrong? Do positive law and morality always coincide or can they sometimes be in conflict with each other? How is one to decide in cases of conflict? Here the daring of Stoic ethics is most conspicuous. No member of the school denied that a positive law is morally right or good only if it agrees with the law of nature and that otherwise it must be regarded as an aberration.

The majesty and power of the natural law are emphasized in Chrysippus' celebrated saying, "The natural law is king over everything, divine and human alike. It must be the authority that determines what is good and what is evil, the leader of men destined to live in communities; it lays down standards for right and wrong, and it does so by commanding what is to be done and forbidding what is not to be done." [10] But where is the natural law to be found? How is it to be recognized? The answer of the older Stoics was that the natural law speaks through reason, the same reason that lays upon men their duties to their families and their economic obligations, that, in general, bids man to be fair and just. By nature, that is, in the light of reason, all men are equal. No one is a slave by nature. There are no natural castes and there is no nobility of birth, for he is free and noble who does the right thing. This is as natural and reasonable as it is to say that men are different and their positions in the world must differ. The Stoics maintained their belief in the face of all the relativism and skepticism which in antiquity even as in modern times appealed to historical observation. There can be no doubt that men at different times and in different places have held different opinions, and Chrysippus, a philosopher learned in history, delighted in collecting examples of historical relativism; but like all other Stoics he was undisturbed by the diversity of the phenomena, for behind all the variety there is agreement at least about the basic issues, the agreement of reasonable men of all times and countries. As Epictetus put it in one of his pithy sayings,[11] the formulation of what is lawful is not the province of fools. Plato, in the *Republic* and in the *Philebus,* had ventured the same opinion.

The younger Stoics heard the voice of the natural law not only in reason but in the human conscience also. I do nothing, Seneca says, on account of opinions commonly held; I do everything for conscience's sake.[12] Such conscience is a natural phenomenon, so to speak, a fact of self-experience of a rational being. It legislates before action and judges afterwards; it is nothing but the expression of man's wish to be at peace with himself, to live according to his nature, the nature of the world. And how could man be at peace with himself, with reason, if he acted against reason? Conscience is the court before which we feel responsible even if undiscovered by others; it is the *daimon* within us, the divine voice that speaks within, our custodian. As such, it is a strictly moral and rational phenomenon. It does not promise any rewards or threaten any punishment except that a man not at peace with himself cannot live. It does not demand shame or repentance but seeks instead to prevent men from feeling them. In short, conscience as the Stoic understands it symbolizes the righteousness of man before the Fall.

If one tries to determine in more detail what it is that reason or conscience tells men, one notices first that the natural law does not give men inalienable and indefeasible rights, as the Age of Enlightenment was wont to imagine, but imposes upon them duties, the duties which they have as cosmopolitans or citizens of the republic of rational men and as citizens of a particular state here and now. Generally speaking, this means that man must always resist any wrong and not connive at it even at the risk of death. This is true of his life within both republics. He must uphold the national law and the international law, for both are derived from the natural law. To treat even the enemy as a human being is one of the highest obligations. Nay, the natural law sets certain limits to political ambitions. War should not lead to the complete destruction of the enemy. There should be neither vanquished nor victor. Nothing is more un-Stoic than Cato's insistence that Carthage be destroyed. To preserve the enemy as a check to one's own ambition is the demand of the Stoic statesman, who, moreover, restricts nationalism and patriotism by submitting them to the scrutiny of moral insight. A Stoic cannot say, "My country, right or wrong." There are things so terrible and shameful, maintains Posidonius, that the wise man will not do them even to save his country.

It seems to be consonant with such an attitude that Stoic philosophy should have had a certain indifference to the various forms of government. Kingship, democracy,

oligarchy are considered to be equally satisfactory con-
stitutions. The judgment passed upon them depends on
the spirit in which those in power govern. It may well
be that for the younger Stoics mixed government, the
combination of democratic and aristocratic principles,
constituted the ideal form of government; but from the
very beginning monarchy too was acceptable to the
Stoics, for in their opinion the course of things in this
world is determined not by institutions but by men. If
the king understands that his reign is nothing but a
glorified service, he is a good king; and he performs well
if he learns to say not "it is my will" but "it is my duty"
and if he knows what is good and evil, if he exercises
self-control, and if he cultivates reason so that he is in-
vincible in arguments and able to discriminate with regard to the advice given him. In other words, the king
must educate himself and must surround himself with
good advisers, cabinet officers, as it were, and a prime
minister. He should seek the intelligent cooperation of
his subjects and should refrain from revolutionary vio-
lence, and he should practise clemency, a clemency which
must be genuine and original with him, not "the tired-out
cruelty of Augustus." [13]

If the king lives up to these duties, he is "the fountain-
head of the law" or, as the favorite Hellenistic theory of
kingship puts it, the "living law"; but in a way every
good man is the living law. The king like the sage reaches
this goal only if he follows and obeys the divine law,
that is, reason. Although the king may be free from legal
coercion, his freedom does not absolve him from his
duties or obligations. Transgression of the law makes him
a tyrant, and a tyrant must be resisted by all good men.
However great his power, he cannot induce the good
man to do what is immoral, for the good man would

rather suffer death. It is not merely passive resistance either that the Stoa advocated but force against the tyrant and removal of him as of a diseased part of the body politic and the body of mankind. In certain circumstances revolution is the only conservative and moral course open to man.

It is true that the Stoa did not consider political duties to be absolute. The sage will not always participate in politics, for he has other duties to perform which to him are equally important, the search for truth and the teaching of philosophy. His preference will be to share in the politics of a state that is progressing in morality or, if he is so fortunate, in the politics of a good state. He may refrain from political activity altogether in a bad state or may do so for private reasons; but in case of conflict, where the reality of the political situation clashes with the moral law, his obligation is absolute. He must do what is right. Ancient and modern critics alike have often accused the Stoics of not participating in politics and of withdrawing from the pressing duties of the day. These critics forget that for the Stoics political life was not the only life in which morality realizes itself and that unlike Plato and Aristotle they did not regard citizenship as the highest obligation of man. In this respect the temper of the Hellenistic age differed radically from that of the classical period.

It is time to turn from this general and incomplete discussion of man's duty to others and to consider his duties to himself in order that we may see how he can become capable of fulfilling his duties within the family, within society, and within the state. The simplest way of formulating this is to say that man must learn virtue. That virtue can be taught none of the Stoics doubted. All of them also believed that it must be taught, that it is not innate in man. Man is man only if educated; otherwise he remains an animal. Everybody can acquire virtue and make "his character the source of life"; [14] but life is short, and it takes a long time to learn, to turn training into nature. Yet, the goal being the highest that man can attain, no effort is too great, for what one learns and thinks and does are the only possessions one can truly call one's own, the only things that are not lost.

In other words, nobody can afford not to philosophize and to become at some time of his life a scholar. Only if he absorbs the right moral theories—and this in turn requires understanding of the principles of logic and of physics—will he be able to face and to resolve the dissension within his soul and outside in real life; only then will he be able to put away opinion and to reach the truth; only then will he become truly human; in the terminology of Stoic professional ethics, only then will he become a true member of "the human profession."

Now the first step to be taken in entering the profession of man is to find a common point of reference for all one's actions. This is the first step in the process of learning human virtue, for philosophy wants only what human nature wants, that is, it wishes to see the general aspect of all human actions. And the first lesson to be learned is that one must find the cause of everything within oneself.[15] Adapting Plato's words[16] one might say: the responsibility is the chooser's; God is free from guilt. Education requires in addition, however, practical training and insight into the individual nature of the learner. Seneca's theory of education is the best expression of the Stoic's concern with the differences in human nature. Nor should one overlook the fact that such training and education cannot be restricted to one year or two but is a lifelong process. No one practising a profession of any kind will ever stop learning and perfecting himself. Why should it be different with the human profession? The manual of Epictetus and the aphorisms of Marcus Aurelius were meant to accompany man through life and to help him improve his knowledge and his nature. Happy is he, said Cleanthes, who at the end of his life at last reaches the goal.

In this process of education by others and of self-education one thing is worth special notice. Stoic morality was not concerned merely with putting moral situations in a general way. As a matter of fact, the Stoic theorist saw few difficulties in this. It is hard, however, to apply the universal rule to particular cases. There are no sharply drawn pictures of the right thing; the outlines and approximations must be clarified. The so-called rules of duties are meant to translate the general propositions into specific terms, and here too the difficulty increases at different levels. If one is faced with an issue between good and bad, the problem may be relatively easy; but when one good is opposed to another or there is a conflict of duties, the decision straightway becomes difficult. When the good and the so-called useful clash, it often seems to be impossible to find a solution. In putting moral alternatives Stoic casuistry celebrated its greatest triumph. The abyss of human nature was explored, and the intricacies of human choice were set forth. Who should be saved in case of a shipwreck? Women and children or those who will certainly contribute to the welfare of mankind? If men are near to starvation and all their supplies are gone, is it permissible to eat human flesh? These are the famous Cynic paradoxes of the Stoa. They are often quoted in order to prove that in the last analysis Stoic moralism was indifferent to the content of moral action; but nothing could be farther from the truth, for all these paradoxes, which emphasize real situations or portray situations that may become real, were meant to show that man must always take responsibility himself, that the choice is his, that he can never find an excuse in external circumstances, and that even in the last extremity of moral action he and his reason must be the sole point of reference.

Another observation of a general nature should be made. Whereas the Old Stoa considered wisdom, moderation, and courage to be virtues in respect to the individual himself and summed up his duties to others as justice, the younger Stoics emphasized the virtue of philanthropy, of *humanitas*, as the truly altruistic virtue. This philanthropy is "a proficiency and benevolence towards all men without distinction." It presupposes the brotherhood of man. Nature has made all of us one family. Nature has implanted in all of us mutual love, says Seneca.[17] We are all members of one body, Cicero explains.[18] We are all brothers, Epictetus holds.[19] This interrelatedness of all men follows from the community of mankind, Philo asserts.[20]

Reading such statements as these, one cannot help seeing the affinity between Stoicism and Christianity. Lactantius in discussing the Stoic conception of philanthropy, the Stoic feeling of obligation to save a man attacked by wild beasts or threatened by fire, can from his own point of view complain only because they do not believe that one must come to the help of the hungry, the thirsty, and those in pain and that they have no compassion.[21] At the very beginning of this essay I argued against denying that the Stoic sage feels with those who suffer, and at the beginning of this last chapter I tried to point out that the Stoics insist on charity as a virtue. To feed the hungry and to clothe the naked is also a Stoic virtue. Those who unlike Lactantius considered Seneca, Musonius, and Epictetus to have been Christians by nature if not by revelation were more nearly right than he was. The identity of ethical standards is indeed striking. The love of our fellow men, that is, "love thy neighbor," the "law written in our hearts," "render unto Caesar the things that are Caesar's and unto God the things that are God's," "what shall it profit a man to gain the whole world and lose his own soul"—these statements and many others are in spirit Stoic and sometimes even in word.

In other respects, of course, there are differences; and much depends on which of the various trends in early Christianity one selects for comparison with Stoic dogma. The Messianic hopes, the attitude of not acting but waiting, the lack of passions glorified by early monks, the putting aside of earthly wealth, early Christian communism—these have no counterpart in Stoic philosophy. If, however, one thinks of the early fathers of the church who believed in happiness in this world and in the progress and perfection here assured by the coming of Christ, if one has in mind that Christianity which was mainly a moral creed and for which the later theological discussions of Trinity and Transubstantiation were not yet of decisive importance, then Stoicism will certainly appear to be a prefiguration of Christianity.

One feature only separates all the various branches of Christian belief from all sects of Stoic philosophy. The Stoics did not glorify the sinner or the outcast. Nor did Stoicism recognize conversion in the Christian sense of the term. That eternity entered time, that a historical moment was decisive in the history of mankind, that a historical fact confirms and assures the validity of an eternal truth, this is a Christian and not a Stoic conviction, for, no matter how strongly the Stoics insisted on the self-revelation of the divine within the human heart, it was still for them the human heart and human reason alone whereby we have access to divine truth.

This being the case, one might well raise a question that was raised by an unknown Platonist of the first or second century A.D., that is, how that virtue which is the quintessence of Stoicism can be realized by human beings.[22] One may well say that ideally speaking all the concentric circles of duties which the Stoa distinguishes are made to coincide. Duty to oneself becomes duty to all others, and love of self becomes love of all men. Very well, the Academic philosopher insists, all this sounds plausible. Self-love turns into benevolence and justice; but this claim "will not stand the test of extreme cases and so save virtue unless the sense of kinship and kindness is absolute—unless man cares as much for every other man, the lowliest and the most distant, as for himself and his own family. And that is notoriously not the fact." It is impossible for the Epicurean to practice justice, for even in his friends he knows only himself; it is impossible for the Stoic to love all men despite his belief that self-love turns into love of others; there is only one way out, Plato's prescription to become as similar to God as possible, to approximate the divine. That is to say that only through the communion with the Transcendent can man become what the Stoa wishes him to be.

This way, however, is closed to the Stoics. Their answer was very much in the spirit of their manly and heroic philosophy. It can be done because it must be done. That the answer was not given lightheartedly and that the Stoics were sensitive to the extent of the demand they made can be seen from a memorable passage of Epictetus':

Be not deceived, it is a general rule that every creature is attached to nothing so much as to its own interest. Whatever then seems to hinder his way to this, be it a brother or a father or a child or the object of his passion or his own lover, he hates, accuses, and curses it. For he naturally loves nothing so much as his own interest and it is this that is father and brother and kinsfolk and country and god to him. At any rate, when the gods seem to hinder us in regard to this, we revile even the gods and overthrow their statues and set fire to their temples, as Alexander ordered the shrines of Asclepius to be burned when the object of his passion died. Therefore, if interest, religion, honor, country, parents, and friends are set in the same scale, then all are safe; but, if interest is in one scale and in the other friends and country and kindred and justice itself, all these are weighed down by interest and lost, for the creature must needs incline to that side where 'I' and 'mine' are; if they are in the flesh, the ruling power must be there and, if in the will, it must be there and, if in external things, it must be there.

If, then, I identify myself with my will, then and only then shall I be a friend and son and father in the true sense, for this will be my interest—to guard my character for good faith, honor, forbearance, self-control, and cooperation, to maintain my relations with others. But if I separate myself from what is noble, then Epicurus' statement is confirmed, which declares that 'there is no such thing as the noble or at best it is but the creature of opinion.' [23]

The Stoics—Pascal, their bitterest enemy and their fairest critic, says—know only the grandeur of man but not his humanity. If one asks whether they were able to realize the grandeur they envisaged, it is hard to give a satisfactory answer, for the historian is unable to see through words into the reality of human existence and the hearts of men from which their deeds derive. That absolute perfection was achieved by any of the Stoic philosophers no one will dare to believe, and yet one must remember the feeling of the Athenians about Zeno which they recorded on stone after his death: "Whereas Zeno of Citium, son of Mnaseas, has for many years been devoted to philosophy and has afforded to all in his own conduct a pattern for imitation in perfect consistency with his teaching, it has seemed good to the people— and may it turn out well—to bestow praise upon him and to crown him with a golden crown according to the law for his goodness and temperance" (Diogenes Laertius, VII, 10–11). One must remember Antigonus Gonatas, the king for whom his kingship was glorified service, Marcus Aurelius, the emperor under whom Rome rallied once more, Sphaerus and Cleomenes, the reformers of Sparta, the Gracchi and Blossius, and Cato the Younger. None of them would have said with Caesar:

> If wrong must be when empire is the prize,
> The noble cause gives glory to the wrong.

Nor would any of them have uttered the despairing words with which Brutus, the Platonist, ended his life,

> O wretched virtue, thou wert but a name,
> And yet I worshipped thee as real indeed;
> But now it seems, thou wert but Fortune's slave.

Nor can respect be denied the few Stoics whose works are preserved entire, Musonius, the gentleman who loved peace and the retired life, the philosopher who cultivated his garden; Seneca, the *grand seigneur* and statesman; and Epictetus, the slave and schoolmaster. Musonius to his contemporaries was a saint. Seneca, to be sure, often acted according to his maxim that "the wise man, in order to accomplish higher ends, will do even what he disapproves and, although he will not give up good morals, will accommodate himself." When he was faced with the ultimate decision, he upheld the spirit of the Stoic teaching. As one reads Epictetus, one does believe his claim that despite all adversities he sings like the nightingale the praises of God. Plutarch, by no means an admirer of

the Stoa, says of men in general that though the Stoic
doctrine tends to make the daring venturesome and may
even mislead them, those whose character is mild and
profound are led by it to their proper moral virtue.[24]

It still may be asked how Stoicism stands the test of
truth. If recent history has taught us anything, it is that
one can meet the test of life and death even for the sake
of wrong principles, for this, it seems to me, is the truly
disturbing fact about Fascism and Communism. Were I
a philosopher in my own right, I should try to answer in
terms of a philosophical world view the question concerning the value of Stoicism; but the historian must restrict
himself to a few historical remarks.

The physics of the Stoics is obviously not only anti-
quated but wrong from the point of view of modern
physics. This is not to say, however, that its problems
have all been resolved and are no longer relevant. What
power shapes an organism and whether physical events
require a teleological explanation are still open questions.
It is safe to say only that the dynamic conception of the
Stoics agrees better with the facts than does the conception of the atom that the Epicureans had; and the Stoic
interpretation of phenomena as events approximates the
modern interpretation of physical phenomena more close-
ly than does any other ancient physical theory.

The similarity between Stoic logic and modern symbolic logic I have mentioned. On the whole, the logical
investigations of the Stoa impress the modern interpreter
because they aim at a system of factual investigation,
whereas Aristotelian logic, being a logic of subsumption
dependent on the existence of transcendent ideas, seems
to us to be reactionary and untrue. It should be remem-
bered also that the Stoic discovery of the central importance of the subject in shaping perception and knowl-

edge has remained the foundation of epistemological analysis. Within the sphere of ancient thought, Stoic subjectivism, Chrysippus' concern with the "I," is the presupposition of Plotinus' idealism.

It is in ethics, however, that the Stoics made their greatest contribution. On this I need not dwell after having discussed the Stoic way of life; and I trust that no further elaboration is required to show why Stoic morality was infused into Christianity, why it was revived in the sixteenth and seventeenth centuries, and why the whole discussion of natural law is a discussion in categories of the Stoa. When in the famous debate on the formulation of the American Constitution Cicero was cited as an important authority on politics, it was really the Stoics who were being cited; and this was right, for their political theory still is, I believe, the political theory most dear to the hearts of all freedom-loving men.

I hasten to add that there are definite limitations even to Stoic ethics. One such limitation we have come to see more clearly, although Pascal had already noticed it. The Stoic put the whole responsibility on the individual and underestimated the importance of institutions. What the climate of opinion may be is not so unimportant as it seemed to be to the Stoics, and Plato was more nearly right when he said that in a disorganized and corrupt state even the philosopher cannot reach the full measure of his being. Moreover, like all ancient thinkers the Stoics underestimated the importance of the moment in human decisions, the creativity of time and history. That there is progress in the sense that in the mysterious nothingness between past and future, which we call now, something unexpected and unconditioned comes into existence— this was first seen by Christian thinkers and in a rationalized form is the basis of existentialism, the philosophy that is most modern because it explicates what man now experiences. Finally one may say, though any Kantian would deny it, that duty alone does not express the fullness of moral obligation, for without love duty is cold; but here the never ending fight about philosophical truth begins, and I must not overstep the limits of my undertaking.

I hope to have shown that the Stoic sage is not the stony similitude of a Platonist; but, if Stoicism be compared with Platonism or Aristotelianism or any kind of idealism, it will be found, I confess, to lack one ingredient: it does not satisfy what Kant called the eternal metaphysical need of man. Whether or not there is an answer to metaphysical questions, the questions are real; and they cannot be interpreted away. In denying transcendence even as a limitative concept Stoicism becomes flat; it makes the world appear two-dimensional instead of three-dimensional, and therefore it indulges itself in a superficial optimism, a superficial trust in reason.

The Stoics unflinchingly believed that reason leads man to the good; but, great as was their merit in emphasizing the importance of practical reason as the distinguishing mark between man and animal, they deceived themselves by further identifying all reasoning with moral insight. Reason can be misused for bad purposes. It may be made to serve bad ends, as Schopenhauer said. Of this truth the Stoics were naïvely unaware. They also fell prey to the illusion of the nineteenth century that evil is nothing but misunderstanding and that enlightenment and change of conditions can restore man to his original good nature. We have learned to our dismay that if there is coolness of moral action and help without sympathy or love, there is also passionless crime, crime for the sake of crime, abetted and supported by reason.

The devil is as real as the angel. The Stoics did not see this, and therefore they also underestimated the significance of suffering or pain, as Schopenhauer pointed out. Externalization of all suffering, if not the necessary consequence of Stoicism, is at least an accidental conclusion that has been drawn from it over and over again.

These animadversions imply no disrespect for the greatness of the Stoic teaching, for one can criticize and still admire. Matthew Arnold was right. Stoicism is somehow the creed of all freedom-loving men. If the divine appears in it in an imperfect form, that does not diminish its value, for all gods conceived by men are but the dim reflections of absolute truth.

NOTES   INDEX

NOTES

I. THE STOIC SAGE

1. *Civitas Dei* 19, 1.
2. H. von Arnim, *Stoicorum veterum fragmenta,* III, p. 6, 15; p. 69, 25; cf. III, 73.
3. *Ibid.*
4. Arnim, I, p. 45, 22.
5. *An Essay on Man* II, 101–103.
6. *Enchiridion* 16.
7. Arnim, I, fg. 215.
8. *De Constantia* X, 4.
9. *De Clementia* II, 6.
10. II, 5.
11. IV, 7, 30.
12. II, 6, 9.
13. Arnim, III, fg. 191.
14. Epicetetus, III, 24, 51.
15. Epictetus, I, 2, 22.
16. E. Bevan, *Stoics and Sceptics,* p. 48.
17. For example, A.-J. Festugière, *Epicure et ses Dieux* (Paris, 1946), pp. 130–131.
18. Epictetus, II, 17, 29; IV, 3, 9.
19. Epictetus, III, 24, 101.
20. Epictetus, III, 24, 97.
21. Epictetus, I, 1, 10.
22. Epictetus, III, 24, 1.
23. Diogenes Laertius, VII, 117.
24. Diogenes Laertius, VII, 123.
25. Marcus Aurelius, III, 7.
26. Arnim, I, fg. 242; cf. Arnim, I, fg. 348.
27. *Odes* III, iii, 7–8.

28. *Epistles* I, 1, 106–108.
29. I, 6, 30.
30. II, 16, 13.
31. Diogenes Laertius, VII, 30.
32. *De Constantia* I, 1.
33. Arnim, I, fg. 234.
34. Cicero, *De Finibus* IV, 20, 56.
35. Arnim, I, fg. 529.
36. Epictetus, *Manual* 50 (51).
37. Bevan, *Stoics and Sceptics,* pp. 26–28.
38. *Ibid.,* p. 32.
39. Demochares, son of Demosthenes, in Athenaeus, VI, 253 C.
40. Theopompus in Jacoby, *Frag. Greek Hist.,* 115 F 224–225.
41. *De Beneficiis* VII, 2, 5.
42. Bevan, *Stoics and Sceptics,* pp. 21–22, 25, 32, and 75.
43. Arnim, I, fg. 54.
44. *De Otio* 5, 6.
45. Arnim, I, fg. 235.
46. Bevan, *Stoics and Sceptics,* pp. 22–23.
47. *Ibid.,* pp. 36, 39, and 42.
48. Diogenes Laertius, VII, 2.
49. Bevan, *Stoics and Sceptics,* pp. 40, 32.

II. THE STOIC CONCEPT OF NATURE

1. *Adv. Math.* IX, 211.
2. Arnim, II, fgs. 937, 275f.
3. Arnim, II, fg. 944.
4. Arnim, II, fg. 946.
5. Arnim, I, fg. 500.
6. Arnim, I, fg. 504.
7. *Metaphysics* 1073, B 4.
8. Arnim, II, fg. 1150.
9. Arnim, II, fg. 1163.
10. Arnim, II, fgs. 1152f.
11. Arnim, II, fg. 1140.
12. Arnim, II, fgs. 1169f.
13. Epictetus, I, 1, 10.
14. Arnim, II, fgs. 1176, 1170, 1178, 1177.
15. *De Usu Partium* XI, 14 (III, pp. 905–906 K.).
16. Arnim, I, fg. 486.
17. Arnim, I, fg. 538.
18. Diogenes Laertius, VII, 84.
19. Arnim, III, fg. 178.
20. Arnim, III, fg. 182.

21. Arnim, III, fg. 188.
22. Arnim, III, fg. 181.
23. Arnim, III, fg. 188.
24. Arnim, III, fg. 184.
25. Arnim, III, fg. 186.
26. *An Essay on Man* II, 93, 87.
27. *Ibid.*, II, 65–66.
28. *Ibid.*, 53–54.
29. *Ibid.*, 107–108.

III.   STOIC SELF-CRITICISM

1. *Epist. Mor.* 33.
2. *Nat. Quaest.* VII, 30, 5.
3. *Nat. Quaest.* VII, 25, 4–5.
4. Seneca, *Epist. Mor.* 78, 28.

IV.   THE STOIC WAY OF LIFE

1. Arnim, III, fg. 351.
2. *Politics* 1260 A 41–B 1.
3. *Politics* 1260 A 36f.
4. Plato, *Laws* 715 C–D.
5. Arnim, III, fg. 689.
6. See Cicero, *De Officiis* III, 51–57 and 89–92.
7. *Politics* 1267 B 13.
8. Cicero, *De Finibus* III, 19, 64.
9. IV, 7, 33f; 1, 12, 7.
10. Arnim, III, fg. 314.
11. IV, 7, 33–34.
12. *Dial.* VIII, 20, 4.
13. Seneca, *De Clementia* I, 11, 2.
14. Arnim, I, fg. 203.
15. Arnim, III, fg. 543.
16. *Republic* 617 E.
17. *Epist. Mor.* 95, 52.
18. *De Finibus* III, 63.
19. I, 13, 3–4.
20. Arnim, III, fg. 436.
21. Arnim, III, fg. 450.
22. *Anonymer Kommentar zu Platons Theatet*, H. Diels and W. Schubart (Berlin, 1905), cols. 5–7; cf. P. Shorey, *Classical Philology*, 24 (1929):509–510.
23. II, 22, 15–21; cf. K. Praechter, *Hermes*, 51(1916):519.
24. *Agis and Cleomenes* 23 (2), 805 E.

INDEX